"Reading Beth Corcoran's book is like peering into the journal of almost any mother of small children. Moms will see themselves in the honest entries in this practical devotional. It offers realistic reflections that are short enough for moms to read, helpful suggestions for application, and one-sentence prayers that moms could actually pray. The short but thought-provoking entries will provide hope, humor, and encouragement to any mom."

—Keri Wyatt Kent
author of *God's Whisper in a Mother's Chaos*

"With tenderness and spiritual insight, Elisabeth shares the joys and frustrations of mothering in a way that is sure to touch your heart. Mom, . . . read and be blessed!"

—Lorraine Pintus
author of *Diapers, Pacifiers & Other Holy Things*
and coauthor of *Intimate Issues*

"*Calm in My Chaos* is a wonderful encouragement for mothers of young children. Elisabeth Corcoran shares her experiences with honesty and sensitivity. Her foundation is Scripture, and the manner in which she takes the Word and weaves it through the experiences of her day will encourage many a mom. A wonderful book."

—Carol Jo Brazo
author of *No Ordinary Home*

Calm in My Chaos

Encouragement for a Mom's Weary Soul

Elisabeth K. Corcoran

kregel
PUBLICATIONS

Grand Rapids, MI 49501

Calm in My Chaos: Encouragement for a Mom's Weary Soul

© 2001 by Elisabeth Corcoran

Published by Kregel Publications, a division of Kregel, Inc., P.O. Box 2607, Grand Rapids, MI 49501. Kregel Publications provides trusted, biblical publications for Christian growth and service. For more information about Kregel Publications, visit our web site: www.kregel.com

Library of Congress Cataloging-in-Publication Data
Corcoran, Elisabeth.
   Calm in my chaos: encouragement for a mom's weary soul / Elisabeth Corcoran.
      p.   cm.
   1. Mothers—Prayer-books and devotions—English.
2. Motherhood—Religious aspects—Christianity—Meditations.
I. Title.
BV4847 .C67   2001   242'.6431—dc21   00-048736
                                                                CIP

ISBN 0-8254-2388-0

Printed in the United States of America

1 2 3 4 5 / 05 04 03 02 01

Contents

Acknowledgments

This book would not be in your hands today if it weren't for my heavenly Father. Thank You, thank You, thank You for allowing me to dream huge and for being my co-Author!

To my husband, Kevin, for basically saying to me, "Why not?!" I want to thank you deeply for your support and for the freedom you have allowed me so that I could find my part in God's abundant plan. I am who I am because you are my husband.

For all of my friends of the heart, new and old, whom I so desperately want to list . . . but where would I begin and end? I thank you for being the eyes, ears, mouths, and hands of Jesus in my life. You make up some of the sweetest parts of my life. The friends in my life are not indulgences—you are my sustenance.

My church body, Blackberry Creek Community Church, who always make me feel that they are glad I am a "hand" and that my place is with them.

For my parents—the foundation you gave me is a big part of who I am today. I am thankful for your part in my life.

For my Grampa Klein—who believed in me so much, he made copies of the early version of this work at Kinko's to pass out to his condo friends and offered to plunk down his savings to see the manuscript published. Thank you.

And, of course, to Sara and Jack—without my inspirations there would have been no tales to tell. Sara and Jack, you are my stories.

My publisher—where would I be without all of you at Kregel Publications? Other than sitting here writing up a list of acknowledgments that only I would ever read! You took my dream and gently made it come to pass. I owe you all my deepest gratitude.

Introduction

At conception, we all are blank slates. But God has plans for each of our lives. Each day is a story. Some tales are filled with remarkable characters. Some are horrors, with gremlins lurking around corners, ready to engulf us. Others are romantic classics. Some are situation comedies. And still others are monologues—one character just trying to make it through the day.

Each one of our lives is a volume, waiting to be shared. God is our Author (and Perfecter), and we are the narrators. We have within us one story after another of a life being lived and a faith being built. Some stories are mundane; some are nothing short of miraculous. Some reveal our successes when we rest in the shadow of His wings; others illustrate our failures when we try to leave God behind and muddle through life on our own terms and in our own strength.

These pages contain some of my stories. I pray that they encourage you as you daily write your own tale as a woman, wife, and mom. I pray that, somehow, reading about my adventures will comfort you and spur you on in yours. Let's take hold of the book of life that we all hold in common and turn the pages together for a while. And I'll share with you how I find moments of calm in my chaos.

Dear Jesus,
Please order our days,
Stretch our hours,
Fill our minutes,
Enlarge our love.
Amen.

Home, Sweet Home

The LORD's curse is on the house of the wicked,
but he blesses the home of the righteous.

—Proverbs 3:33

ome for some means freedom. To others it is security; to yet others it is a money pit. To some of us our home is our shelter, haven, and refuge. My home with my husband, Kevin, is all of those to me. This home was a gift from our heavenly Father, and I am forever grateful. And I want to dedicate my home to Him. This prayer of dedication is for all of us who love our homes—as is—for what they mean to our souls.

Father, thank You for a sunlit kitchen all my own. I ask that this room be a source of health, hospitality, and love. May we feel You here. Thank You for a cozy living room all my own. I ask that this room be a haven for my family and friends and a continual place of peace and relaxation. May we feel You here. Thank You for a beautiful bedroom all our own. I ask that only romantic, precious, love-filled moments be shared here. May we feel You here. Thank You for our children's rooms. I ask that these rooms be used for special moments with our daughter and son. I ask that You fill these rooms with Your love and care. May we feel You here. May warm memories be held in these walls. May we see the legacy that You are helping us build. And may we always strive to be worthy of the blessing of this home that You have provided for us. Amen.

Personal Touch

No matter what shape your home is in, one of your roles as a woman is to create a place of shelter for your family. Think of one idea you can implement today to create that atmosphere—quiet music playing throughout the day, candlelit dinner for the entire family, or the kids playing quietly when your husband gets home so he's not bombarded with chaos.

> *I will be careful to lead a blameless life—*
> *when will you come to me?*
> *I will walk in my house*
> *with blameless heart.*
>
> —Psalm 101:2

Prayer

Dear Father, thank You for the place You allow me to call home. May I remember always that it is a gift from You and that I need to respond accordingly. Help me to walk blamelessly in my home as I offer it to You as a dwelling place. May I and my family feel You here. Amen.

2

The Days Before Sara's Birth

Letters to God

16 Days Before

[S]he trusts in the LORD;
let the LORD rescue [her].
Let him deliver [her],
since [s]he delights in him.
—Psalm 22:8

And to think you were midwife at my birth,
setting me at my mother's breasts!
When I left the womb you cradled me;
since the moment of birth you've been my God.
—Psalm 22:9–10 *The Message*

What a blessing these words of comfort are! You, Father, will be my midwife. And You, Father, are already Sara's God. Thank You!

13 Days Before
The earth is the LORD's, and everything in it.
—Psalm 24:1

I am God's.
Kevin is God's.
Sara is God's.
Because He made us. Because He designed us.
Because He put us together before there was time.
Because He loves me more than anyone else ever could.
Therefore, He does, and will, take care of us.
Completely.

11 Days Before

Lord, I want Your perfect will to be done regarding the length and pain and work and circumstances of labor and delivery of Sara. You know I want an easy, fast, uncomplicated, rewarding delivery; but I know if You're with me, I can do all things.

Thank You in advance for being with me now, and then. Help me trust that You care for all the details of this baby's birth, from the first contraction to her first cry. Amen.

10 Days Before

Father, once again I give You the cares and concerns I have regarding the birth. I trust that Sara will be born precisely at the time You ordained for Your purposes. I ask that You help me relax during my labor. I mean deep relaxation—not scared, not tense, and not stressed.

Help me to grow in my faith that I may be a godly example to this child. May Kevin and I lead her to a saving knowledge of Christ.

Prepare my heart, soul, mind, and body for the awesome tasks before me: labor and delivery and godly motherhood. Amen.

9 Days Before

Father, give me heavenly eyes to fully appreciate the baby You are creating inside of me. I confess all my fears to You and cast them upon You. I receive Your deliverance from these fears, knowing that fear cannot dwell in Your perfect love. Amen.

8 Days Before

Father, I praise You, knowing that You are preparing me for the arrival of my child. Thank You for the sweetest human experience thus far in my life. Carrying this baby has been as close to perfection as I've ever felt in my life. And it was a gift from You.

I come to You again asking that You will be with me during the birthing process—guiding, strengthening, and comforting me and my baby. And please enable and empower Kevin to handle the task of coaching and supporting me. Amen.

6 Days Before

Well, Lord, I threw up this morning. It's any time now, isn't it? We're really having a baby! I am still in shock, denial, and awe!

Father, I know You haven't brought me this far to leave me. I know that our baby will be delivered in Your perfect timing and in Your perfect way.

Help me to realize that You do not give me a spirit of fear—that fear and anxiety do not come from You—but instead You have given me a spirit of power, love, and peace.

Can this attitude change really be happening? Can I truly be looking forward to these upcoming challenges? Is my fear really easing? Please keep working on my heart, soul, mind, and body, Father. Amen.

4 Days Before

Encouragement from my best friend, Keely: "Let this be your victory chant," she said, "'I can do all things through Him who strengthens me' (Phil. 4:13 NASB)."

3 Days Before

By Thee I have been sustained from my birth;
Thou art He who took me from my mother's womb.
—Psalm 71:6 NASB

Today's my due date! But I don't think it really will be. So I'm going to go on as if nothing is different. I receive the assurance that my time and my baby's due date are in Your hands.

Help me, Father, to avoid confusion by keeping my mind centered on You. Bless me with self-control and peace so that I may pray during labor and delivery.

I want to dedicate my baby's birth to You. I want people to see my peace. I want Kevin and me to truly feel Your hand upon us. Help us to know that we can bravely look this experience in the eye and confidently face it head on. I want labor, not just the birth, to be a joyful and holy event.

You're blessing us with Sara; I now ask that You bless Sara with us. Help us to be worthy of the gift and opportunity of parenthood.

We are beginning a new generation where Christ is truly our foundation and Yahweh is truly our God and Father. Don't let us ever take this lightly. Always remind us. Amen.

1 Day Before

I seem to be leaking something. I'm hoping it's amniotic fluid. Can this get any more glamorous? I think I'll be in labor tomorrow. Something is going on inside my body. Thank You for having Your hand on the circumstances of the next few days. Help us both to not worry but to trust in You. May Your unfailing love be my comfort. Amen.

The Day Of

2:36 A.M.: Sara Taylor Corcoran miraculously entered this world and our lives.

Personal Touch

If you haven't already, get yourself a journal and write down as much as you can remember about the moments before, during, and after the birth of your child. You will want to retell this story for years to come.

Prayer

Heavenly Father, I will never be able to thank You enough for my beautiful and perfect daughter. But with my life, I will try. Amen.

3

The Human Body

I can do all things through Him
[Christ] who strengthens me.
—Philippians 4:13 NASB

"I am such a wimp." "I am completely uncoordinated."
"I have absolutely no tolerance for pain." These are statements that I once used to describe myself. I was always chosen last in PE. In fact, I even faked being sick to get out of gym. I took two aspirin if I thought I might be on the verge of a headache. I did not like discomfort. I had no confidence in my body and its abilities.

But something changed. On April 1, 1996, I discovered that I was pregnant. If pregnancy does not take your body on a physical roller coaster, nothing will. The realization that I had another human body living and growing inside me produced the daunting understanding that this other human body would somehow have to emerge from my human body. Over the next months, thoughts of fear and uncertainty plagued me as I agonized over how the task of birth would truly play out for me.

After being given the "sex talk" in fifth grade, I decided to never have children if that were the only way to get them. As I got older, I decided that I did want children, but I would demand every drug that was legal and, if possible, some not-so-legal, starting preferably sometime in the eighth month just to be safe. However, the thought of drug relief did not completely allay my concern of the prospect of labor and delivery.

Then halfway through the pregnancy, my husband suggested that we give birth using the Bradley method. For those of you who aren't familiar with this, the Bradley method is drug-free. Fantastic. Not only was I giving birth to another person, but when she came out I would be completely aware of the situation.

As the months flew by and our Bradley classes educated us, my trepidation waned. My husband and I trained like athletes, exercising and practicing relaxation and labor sessions. By my eighth month, I actually looked forward to the challenge before me.

The day finally came. In the evening I felt the first contraction. My uterus was tightening around my daughter every six minutes with manageable intensity. "So far, so good," I thought. But as the minutes sped by and the contractions became more concentrated, my composure began to fall apart. I felt out of control of my body, and all my anxieties rushed back. "I cannot do this," became my chant. By the time we reached the hospital, I was an hour away from pushing. The contractions were waves of pain that washed over every inch of my body. The waves kept coming and I had no break from them. When it was time to push, I mustered up every ounce of energy and strength as I begged for this saga to end. With each push I came one minute closer to meeting my precious daughter. And then she arrived! I had done it!

In truth, my humanness was apparent. I screamed with pain and the tearing of muscles, but what empowerment comes with accomplishment! I learned that my body was capable of much more than I had given myself credit for. I had never considered myself an athlete, but after this triumph, there was no denying that I could run with the best of them. My confidence was back tenfold. You will never hear the phrase "I am a wimp" come from my lips again.

Personal Touch

It takes courage to be a parent, whether parenting the children born to you or those you have adopted and love as your own. You've met the challenge of becoming a parent—of this you can be proud. Think of the courage you've gained through this experience. How has this equipped you to meet the many challenges you face in your life?

For you created my inmost being;
you knit me together in my mother's womb.
I praise you because I am fearfully and wonderfully made;
your works are wonderful,
I know that full well.

—Psalm 139:13–14

Prayer

Dear heavenly Father, thank You for bringing me through that magical experience—as painful as it was. It was a gift from You because it resulted in my child. Grant me times of rest as I adjust to this amazing responsibility and to give my body a chance to heal or my mind a chance to let this all sink in. Give me wisdom to rest, no matter how good I may feel or how many things need to be done. May I never forget that through Your strength I was able to open my heart to this precious being! Amen.

4

Shades of the Flood

For I have learned to be content whatever the circumstances.
I know what it is to be in need, and I know what it is to
have plenty. I have learned the secret of being content
in any and every situation.

—Philippians 4:11–12

orty days or sixteen hours, it's all about the same to me. I am watching rain fall from my window. I have developed a love/hate relationship with rain over the past few months. I love it because I know that rain was made for a purpose. But I hate it (and am slightly scared of it now) because my husband and I were affected by a flood. Other families in our area were hit much harder by this disaster. We didn't lose our home. We just lost some belongings: carpet and tile, our refrigerator, our furnace, our cars, and our savings. But after four weeks of living elsewhere, we were able to move back into our home.

The fact remains though, we did lose something and I'm still trying to deal with it. We were expecting our first child, and it was our dream to move out of our small (and I mean *small*) house and into something a little bigger. We had saved and waited for the "right" moment to start a family. We found the home we wanted, in the town we wanted, and in our price range. We were in the process of buying this home—signed contract and all. But along came the flood. Sixteen hours of rain. We have not been able to sell our home. Even if we did sell it, now we can't afford a new one. The flood took away our dream of a bigger home for our new family.

What have I learned? What am I still learning? I am trying to find contentment in any circumstance. On the morning of the flood, as I stood in my living room watching the water cover my feet, I repeated to myself, "Beth, you *must* act out your beliefs. God loves us and cares for us and has all of this in His hands. You *must* live what you believe. You have no other choice." But I must admit, at first I had some bad moments. Why would God take away all we had dreamed of? We had been so responsible and planned for so long. What had we done wrong? Two truths have occurred to me: bad things *do* happen to "good" people, but they don't happen without cause. Unfortunately, I have yet to find the cause. Some have said, "God must not have wanted you to buy that other house." That may be true, but it has not burned down or spontaneously combusted—it is still sitting there, waiting for another family to call it home. But I think the reason this all happened is simply because God is God. He wants me to want no more than Him. And until then, until I am able to say with complete honesty that "I am content in every circumstance," I will be staying in these current circumstances.

And what is more—even beyond that—maybe God wants

me here. Right where I am in this small house. Just because. Not as a punishment. Not because I am not doing something right enough or well enough or holy enough. Not because my service isn't all it should be. And not because my quiet times sometimes leave something to be desired. God doesn't work that way. Maybe He just wants me here. This is the home He wants for me and my family. And that is what I am doing my best to accept. Besides, I don't really need to host overnight guests or a Thanksgiving dinner anytime soon.

But just you wait. When I get to heaven I am going to have a fireplace, a porch with a swing, and a second bathroom. It will be great. And I'll invite everyone I know to come over for dinner.

Personal Touch

Life sometimes comes unraveled. But the bad is as much a part of our tapestry as the good. As we come to accept both, we come to see that they both offer us so much and teach us such great lessons about life and God's love for us.

> *When times are good, be happy;*
> *but when times are bad, consider:*
> *God has made the one*
> *as well as the other.*
> —Ecclesiastes 7:14

Prayer

Dear Father, thank You for lessons that comfort and lessons that hurt. Both teach, both bring about growth and dependence on You, and that is Your goal for me. Let it be mine as well. Amen.

Author's Note

The summer after writing this, one year after the flood, we were able to move to a great home. Fireplace, check. Porch, check. Swing, still waiting on that one. Second bathroom, currently under construction. Seems that God wants me *here* now.

5

Oh, How I Remember

Create in me a clean heart, O God;
and renew a right spirit within me.
—Psalm 51:10 KJV

Today I received a package in the mail from a friend. Books! *Books.* I remember books. They have hard covers and pages so crisp they sometimes stick together—pages filled with words just waiting to be discovered. It's been awhile, but I used to read a good book in one sitting. That's when "one sitting" equaled two or three hours. The only books I read in one sitting these days begin with the words, "The cow says MOOO!" Yes, I remember books. I remember a lot of things about my "old" life. But one thing I can't recall is my heart. I don't remember what my heart was like before I became Sara's mommy.

It's interesting, this "being a Christian." I've felt that it was "wrong" to talk about how very much I adore my child. Christians believe that the husband should come before the children. I believe that. But I've found that I'm not called to love my husband *more* than my child; I should love them differently. And I do. The motto "love is a choice" is, every now and then, a reality in marriage (no offense, Kevin). But with Sara, I have no choice. My heart just loves her. So maybe I can't run to the mall whenever I want. And now it takes me a couple of months to get through a book that has more than ten words. But my heart has been forever changed. And that's not a bad trade.

Personal Touch

After the birth of a child you may notice that your time and priorities have changed forever. But if you haven't noticed yet, you will soon—the changes are amazingly well worth it.

These changes, though, may leave you feeling drained. You need to realize up front that it is more than okay to take some time to fill yourself so that you can be all that your child needs.

So buy yourself a book, or supplies to work on a project or hobby, and set aside fifteen minutes each day this week to spend on it. You deserve to continue pursuing your pre-child interests.

> *Restore to me the joy of your salvation*
> *and grant me a willing spirit, to sustain me.*
> —Psalm 51:12

Prayer

Dear Father, please remind me today of all the treasures I have in this child. Thank You for new interests to fill a new season and new eyes to see my new life. Amen.

6

The Parable of Your Talents

For a dream comes through much activity.
—Ecclesiastes 5:3 NKJV

*A*re you familiar with the parable of the talents? (You will find this story in Matthew 25:14–29.) A talent was once thought to be a unit of measure. Later, a talent was the name for a form of money worth more than $1,000. On the surface, the parable of the talents is about some men who invested, saved, and buried *money*. But I like to think that Jesus might have been talking about our actual talents—*our gifts*. God gives each of us talents and gifts.

It has taken me over ten years to identify my gifts and to believe that they come literally from God. I enjoy writing and do it well. I don't say that with pride *or* modesty, but with the realization that writing is one of the talents that God has given to me. I don't know if this gift is yet professional enough to offer to the world. Regardless, my job is not to bury it in the ground. It's not my role to judge what is good enough or who should be my audience. It's my job to hone my skills and use them to the best of my ability, then trust God to let the chips fall where they may.

So what am I trying to say? Go for it! You have at least one talent that you do really, really well and that you really, really enjoy doing. God gave it to you for a reason. Use that talent. Don't bury it in your figurative ground. It's easy to sit around dreaming big dreams and never take steps to accomplish them. But we need to face reality. We only get one life. We can't say, "This life I'll be the wife and mom. And in my next life, that's when I'll write a book (or start a women's group, or reach out to the homeless, or take art lessons, or finish my master's, etc.)." *This* is our chance. Maybe God is the One who placed those dreams—regardless of how impossible they may seem—in your heart in the first place.

Personal Touch

What is your passion? What do you love doing? Spend some time today jotting down all of your strengths, interests, and hobbies. Then choose one or two to develop by either taking a class, reading a book, or spending time with someone else who enjoys the same things. Now that you're in the honing process, how are you going to use *your* talent for God?

> *"If you can?" said Jesus. "Everything is*
> *possible for him who believes."*
> —Mark 9:23

Hide not your talents,
They for use were made.
What's a sundial in the shade?
       —Benjamin Franklin

Prayer

Dear heavenly Father, thank You for blessing me with talents. If I haven't yet figured out what they are, please bring me clarity and creativity. If I know clearly how You have gifted me, please show me ways in which I can be used to further Your kingdom, bring You glory, and find fulfillment. Take my dreams, Jesus, and only give them back if that's what You want. I give over my dreams as a sacrifice of praise. Amen.

7

Mission Incredible

"For I know the plans I have for you," declares the LORD,
"plans to prosper you and not to harm you, plans to give
you hope and a future."

—Jeremiah 29:11

I want to live purposely. I don't want my days to simply carry me with the ebb and flow of life as I sit back and watch. God has given me this life, with these unique circumstances and my unique gifts, and I want to give back to Him by living my life *on purpose.*

Have you ever sat down and mapped out a personal mission statement? I spent some time awhile ago reading and working through a wonderful Bible study titled *Designing a Woman's Life.* Judith Couchman struck a chord when she wrote that to pursue one's purpose is "to discover our God-intended reason for being and to design our lives accordingly."[1]

I know what you're thinking. "I'm too busy to design my life. I don't even have time to eat out with my husband let alone the time to establish a unique purpose and mission statement." Well, that is exactly what I want for you. I want you to spend some time in prayer and in thought about what gets you excited. Then mold it into a mission statement that becomes the driving force behind your daily choices.

According to Judith Couchman, our purposes in life are to "live in God's presence, make the world better, and use our talents." How do those purposes fit into your life right now?

I can't tell you what your mission statement may look like. But I can share with you how I constructed mine.

I have decided, through prayer and an honest search of my heart and gifts, that my purpose is *to encourage women through creative word and love-driven deed in their life's journey with God.* This can be an umbrella that covers many areas for me:

- I can minister as Christ would to my husband and children so that all women see Him working in my family.
- I can directly minister to women within my women's ministry as I lead and coordinate with a servant's heart.
- I can directly minister to my closest friends and family with encouragement and love through unselfish time and prayer spent on and with them.
- I can minister to a general audience as my words are published.

A friend, who has never even seen my mission statement, wrote the following to me:

B-ringing women together
E-ncouraging
T-heir
H-earts for Home and Him

When you are living out your mission, it is quietly evident to those around you. And that is amazing encouragement and validation from God Himself.

Personal Touch

I encourage you to spend some time in the next few days considering what your talents are. Then think about how you feel God wants you to use them in light of the three purposes in life.

> *Live creatively, friends. . . . Make a careful*
> *exploration of who you are and the work you*
> *have been given, and then sink yourself into*
> *that. Don't be impressed with yourself. Don't*
> *compare yourself with others. Each of you*
> *must take responsibility for doing the creative*
> *best you can with your own life.*
> —Galatians 6:1, 3–5 *The Message*

Prayer

Dear Father, thank You for placing within me the desire to live with a goal in mind. Please grant me the wisdom, discernment, and clarity to focus myself as I weave my own personal, unique mission statement. Work in my heart and life that I may honor and glorify You with my actions. Amen.

8

The Whole Point

*For God so loved the world [you] that he gave his one
and only Son, that whoever believes in him shall not perish
but have eternal life.*

—John 3:16

I would be remiss if I didn't mention something here. At
this point, you have read a few of my stories. Maybe you've
laughed a little or teared up a bit, but if nothing else, you've
likely related in some way. But I cannot continue without
saying something that makes this whole journey worthwhile.

I want to talk about presents. Presents are wonderful.
Think about the most favorite and treasured gifts that you
have ever been given. What made those gifts so special? A
girlfriend gave me a CD of a singer I love and a book by a
favorite author. I treasured that present. It showed me that
she knew me well enough to give me items I would really
enjoy.

And recently, I had the opportunity to go away for a
weekend by myself. A friend of mine knew I was doing

this. Despite her very busy schedule, she made me a basketful of muffins and brought it to me right before I left. I appreciated this gift because it showed that she was thinking about me and cared for me.

What makes a gift truly special is receiving it from someone who loves you and knows you, and who gives you gifts that you enjoy and need.

Who knows you better than God? No one. He created you. And I don't just mean He created the very first man and woman. He created *you*. He had a wonderful time coming up with the idea of you. And not only does He know you better than anyone else—He loves you more than anyone else does. So He is the Provider of all of the good and perfect gifts in your life.

And He has the most perfect gift to offer to you—Jesus. He knows you well enough to know that you need salvation. He knows you well enough to know you would enjoy abundant life. And He loves you so much that He offers you this gift—His one and only Son—that you might experience salvation and enjoy the gift of life lived to its fullest.

You don't automatically gain the gift of salvation simply because it has been offered to you. And you can't get it by going to church each Sunday, or by being raised in a religious home by religious parents, or by volunteering once a week at a shelter, or by giving 10 percent of your money to the church and other charities. You must *accept* and *receive* the gift yourself.

Picture this: A dear friend gives you a gift for no special reason other than she wanted to. She picked out such a wonderful gift that she could hardly wait to give it to you. She wrapped it beautifully and put a gorgeous gold bow on it. She hands it to you. You say thank you and set it down, then go on about your business. Her feelings are hurt, of course, because of the time and thought she put into the gift, but she doesn't say anything because she's that kind of friend. The gift continues to sit, completely wrapped, on your dining room table for weeks. You send a thank you note to your friend, expressing your gratefulness for her time and how pretty the package has made your home. You occasionally do things for this friend in hopes of repaying her for her gift to you—the gift that has remained unopened.

Now, of course, this has probably never happened. And it sounds ridiculous. Or does it? How many of us have taken the gift that God has offered to us in Jesus and politely put it aside? We have heard of Him. We may even believe He really existed and is God's own Son. We are grateful for Jesus. And we "do things" for God in hopes of repaying Him. But for what? The gift for you is still unopened. You need to open the gift and receive Jesus into *your* heart, trusting Him as *your* personal Savior and Lord.

Personal Touch

We need to realize that God loves us so much and knows us so well that He sent His Son to take away our sin. What a gift!

> *That if you confess with your mouth, "Jesus is Lord," and believe in your heart that God raised him from the dead, you will be saved.*
> —Romans 10:9

Prayer

Dear Jesus, I know that I am a sinner. I know that the only way to enter into heaven and secure eternal life is by believing in You and receiving You. I ask You, Jesus, to come into my heart and life. Thank You for loving me so much that You came to die for *me*. Thank You for taking away my sin. Help me always to remember what a gift You are and what You have done for me. Amen.

Author's Note

If you have just prayed this prayer, you have become a Christian, a follower of Christ, and have been adopted into God's family as His child. Angels are rejoicing! Write me and tell me so I can rejoice, too. (My e-mail address can be found on page 153.) Welcome to the family.

9

Song of a Mother, Wife, and Woman

I fill
My days are consumed with babies, babies
I serve them from within
Even when I find myself lacking
The strength to go on

I fill
My nights are set aside—
Time with husband though
Seems to elude, as there is always something that
Needs doing

I fill
Me, and when?
I must go on, life never slows
Despite what life throws my way
It all goes on

I fill and I fill
But Who fills me
When I find
That all that is left are a few tears
And a few scattered dreams?

You fill and You fill
And I am found able to do
What You call
With abundance and with grace
And knowing Your timing is all that really matters

Personal Touch

Make it a daily choice and priority to spend time being filled up with God's provisions through prayer, reading the Bible, and/or listening to worshipful music. You'll find that you have enough resources to pour yourself out for the ones you love.

> *May the God of hope fill you with all joy and*
> *peace as you trust in him, so that you may*
> *overflow with hope by the power of the*
> *Holy Spirit.*
> —Romans 15:13

Prayer

Dear Father, keep me focused. Keep me balanced. I want to serve You, my husband, and my child(ren), but I ask that You fill me continually with Your joy so I don't become overwhelmed and weary. Give me Your rest, Father. Amen.

10

I Want More!
(Kids)

I appeal to you . . . in the name of our Lord Jesus Christ,
that all of you agree with one another so that there may be
no divisions among you and that you may be perfectly
united in mind and thought.
—1 Corinthians 1:10

*M*ost of my life, I didn't want children. It wasn't just labor that scared me, the entire process of bearing and raising children frightened me. About the time I went to college and fell in love with my then-future husband, my ideas began to change. I was given the opportunity to spend time with a young family of four children. In this case, it was a good thing. I fell in love with the kids and saw how happy they made their parents. I realized I wanted that in my life someday. Though I was still leery, I toyed with the notion of being mom to *one* child. My boyfriend, however, believed in having at least two, so "he or she doesn't turn out like you," he'd say in semi-jest, referring to my only-child status. I knew that we would need to work through this issue before marriage.

Slowly, my desire for children grew until two years into my marriage, when I discovered I was pregnant. The period of my pregnancy was nothing short of miraculous perfection. I felt better physically and emotionally than I had ever felt, and I was in awe of having another human being growing and moving inside of me. My experience of natural childbirth was, though painful, also miraculous and empowering. The minute my daughter left my body, I wanted to be full again, and I was immediately saddened by the emptiness.

My desire for an unending pregnancy was surprising but not unexpected, as I had read many times that women often miss the feeling of attachment that comes from pregnancy. I tried to ride out these feelings, waiting for them to disappear. Four months later, the feelings were still present—wanting to be pregnant, wanting to give birth, wanting to mother over and over again. My heart's desire was to have as many children as possible. (These were obviously the thoughts of a mother who had an immobile infant who slept approximately eighteen hours a day.)

Immediately, I addressed the issue with my husband, assuming he would be thrilled that I had come around to his way of thinking. One day, Kevin asked, "What are you thinking?" "Oh," I said, "how I can't wait to get pregnant again! Can't you?" "Actually," he said, "I was just thinking how being an only child isn't that bad after all." I was unpleasantly surprised to find out that one child was about all he thought he could handle. It seemed that he felt the responsibility of raising a child on a different level than I did. He focused on the practical side—the money and time and sacrifices it would take. I saw the other side—the love and joy we would experience with each child.

We've talked and discussed and argued. This isn't the type of subject one can easily compromise on; you can't have half a child or raise it for ten years and be done. No understanding has yet been reached, though I would settle for one more. My ache will pacify with time and, who knows, may even disappear once my daughter discovers she can flush my car keys down the toilet.

Personal Touch

As you probably figured out, this story takes place post-Sara and pre-Jack. My husband eventually came around, but only after I learned to back off. Are you and your husband struggling with a major issue or difference of opinion right now? If I may make a suggestion, you would be amazed at what can happen if you step back a bit and pray instead of repeatedly pressing your opinion. Easier said than done, I know, but I dare you to try it.

Aim for perfection, listen to my appeal, be of one mind, live in peace. And the God of love and peace will be with you.
—2 Corinthians 13:11

Prayer

Dear Father, please unify my husband and me. Bring peace to any tension You may see. Build up our oneness and remind us both that we're in this journey together. Thank You for my husband. Amen.

11

The Heart of a Mother

Blessed is the [woman] who perseveres under
trial, because when [she] has stood the test,
[she] will receive the crown of life that God has
promised to those who love him.

—James 1:12

I just got home from a family get-together at a restaurant. My mother was holding my eight-month-old daughter and showing her off to some friends. Sara was fussing a little, and as I slowly approached her, she looked in my direction. She focused on my face for a second or two, then she stopped crying and broke out into a beautiful grin. "So? Kids smile all the time. What's the big deal?" The big deal is that my presence not only calmed her, but in seconds it changed her demeanor from one of frustration to one of happiness. She responded to me as if to say, "I know that face. That is the face I see every day. That is the face of someone who takes care of me and anticipates my needs. That is the face of someone who loves me." A tear came to my eye, as it does several times a day when I revel in the miracle that is Sara.

Throughout my life I have tasted abundantly the sweetness of human love. I have been blessed with family and friends. I have a husband who loves me and reminds me of it often through word and deed. I have also given intense devotion to the people I love. But when it comes to love, until I saw that " + " on a little stick last year, I didn't know the half of it.

Sara amazes me more and more with each new day. She has taught me that I have God-given instincts that I never would have believed until now. Holding someone else's new baby used to make me nervous. Yet, there I was, changing her diaper for the first time in the dark at midnight— just me and my twenty-one-hour-old daughter—and you would have thought I had been holding her all my life. It was as if being nervous had not even occurred to me. There was no place for nervousness. There was no room for doubt. I was her mother. *I* was the mother now.

Sara lights up when I begin our prayers. With her tiny hand grasping my finger, and with my simple "Dear Jesus . . ." it's like she knows—as though she understands that we're going into the presence of Someone really wonderful. (OK, so she smiles after a good burp, too, but that's beside the point.) But Sara already has, I believe, tapped into her spiritual nature. When I catch her staring at the dancing flame of a candle, I can tell that her mind is spinning. Sara is already a pensive little girl. She will spend her nights dreaming and her days figuring out how to realize those dreams. I can just tell.

The moment in the restaurant caused me to wonder, do we think of the face of God in this way? Does the mere thought of our heavenly Father instantly change our countenances because we know Him from spending time with

Him every day; because we know He not only meets our needs, but anticipates them even before *we* know what they are; because we know He *knows* us; because we know He loves us so much that He continually puts Himself aside?

Oh, my precious Sara, thank you for awakening in me a new kind of love—a love that shows me a clearer picture of the love God has for me. May I spend my days returning the favor by clarifying what is most important in this life: that I, as your mommy, love you with all my heart—but, sweetheart, God loves you infinitely more.

And I am praying for all of you who strive along with me to earn the title of mother—and the crown.

Personal Touch

What love we have been given! As soon as you finish reading, put this book down and give your child(ren) a wonderful, big, soft, long hug.

> *And when the Chief Shepherd appears,*
> *you will receive the crown of glory that will*
> *never fade away.*
> —1 Peter 5:4

Prayer

Dear Father, today leaves me praying that I am constantly earning the title of Mother. I pray that, as my child sees me today as her provider, I am capable of pointing her toward her true Provider. Thank You for enabling me to be an example of Jesus today. Amen.

12

Where Did She Go?

She sets about her work vigorously;
her arms are strong for her tasks.
—Proverbs 31:17

*H*ave you ever said to yourself, "There's *got* to be more than this! I have just cleaned cranberry juice off the floor for the sixth time today. And I don't know the last time I wore something other than my college sweatshirt! And when did the dog *truly* become my best friend?" You begin to wonder how this all happened. What choices did you make, what steps did you take, what paths did you travel that led you here? When I say "here," what am I referring to? "Here" is the place where you feel like you've lost most of yourself—what you remember yourself to be only a few short years (or even months) back—that intelligent, coherent woman who could get through a conversation without discussing her child's various excretions. *Where did that woman go?* Don't despair, we all feel that way every now and then. And "she" didn't go anywhere. She has just changed. She *is* there underneath the spit-up and sweatshirt. And believe it or not, she knows a whole lot more than you're giving her credit for!

Personal Touch

No matter how old your child(ren), odds are that cabin fever sets in from time to time. Make plans to leave the house without—are you sitting down?—the baby. Go on a date with your husband—you remember him. Or meet a friend for lunch or even run to the mall. The time away will help to recharge your emotional and physical batteries.

> *She is clothed with strength and dignity;*
> *she can laugh at the days to come.*
> *She speaks with wisdom,*
> *and faithful instruction is on her tongue.*
> *She watches over the affairs of her household*
> *and does not eat the bread of idleness.*
> *Her children arise and call her blessed;*
> *her husband also, and he praises her.*
> *—Proverbs 31:25–28*

Prayer

Dear Father, enable me to see the holiness in my position as mother. Help me to see that, though I've changed, I have value simply as a creation and child of Yours. And be my Validator—the Person in my life who helps me see that I am significant. Amen.

13

Second Mother's Day

All the days ordained for me
were written in your book
before one of them came to be.
—Psalm 139:16

I love being a mom. I really love being *Sara's* mommy. It helps that she is one amazing little girl. This year I celebrate my second Mother's Day. I am anticipating my second child's arrival as well. Way back when, I thought being a mother of one was going to be so very difficult. I have a feeling, though, that I have been traveling down easy street this whole time and have a roller coaster ride ahead of me.

Why do we celebrate Mother's Day? One day a year we pay tribute to the women who are caretakers of children's lives and hearts. Technically, I fit the bill. I have kept Sara from a couple of accidents over the months. (Unfortunately, I have been the cause of another few, but we won't get into that.) And I hope that I am forming a curiosity about Jesus in her little soul that will grow as the years go on. I am proud of both of those achievements. But I don't feel worthy just yet of being honored on this day. Because I have so far to go.

A part of me would love to peek into the future in order to be sure that Sara gets through life physically unscathed, emotionally whole, and trusting in Jesus. But I can't know those things now. And it's probably best if I don't. Because if I knew the outcome was as I hope, I wonder if I would do things differently—maybe cut myself some slack and let some important things go. But since I don't know the future, I pour my life into hers, hoping that God gives me the guidance, wisdom, patience, and love that I need to help her find her way to Him.

And when that day comes, that is when I will celebrate Mother's Day. And I will imagine my heavenly Father saying, "Well done."

To all of you who are doing your best to lead your children to Him who loves them even more than you possibly can, I'd like to say "Happy Mother's Day" every day. Keep up the good work.

Personal Touch

Today, this day, this moment, focus on your child. What does your child need emotionally? physically? spiritually? While you don't know what the future holds, you can still put forth your best efforts today.

> *Now we see but a poor reflection as in a*
> *mirror; then we shall see face to face. Now I*
> *know in part; then I shall know fully, even as*
> *I am fully known.*
> —1 Corinthians 13:12

Prayer

Dear Father, You have ordained each day of my baby's life. I am grateful that You are in charge. Help me remember at all times that You hold my child's days and I am simply the caretaker for now. Amen.

14

Sara Discovers

The heavens declare the glory of God;
the skies proclaim the work of his hands.

—Psalm 19:1

I spend 99 percent of my time entrenched in little things. The big picture of this amazing journey that God has allowed each of us passes me by with little thought or wonder on my part. Today, I allowed myself to revel in that other 1 percent. And boy, did I revel. I watched my daughter play in our backyard. Of course she's been in our backyard before. And I have been there with her before, supervising. But today, I *watched* her. I really just watched her. I observed her toddle along and take on our yard as if it were a jungle. Everything is so new to an eighteen-month-old. I watched her discover the awesome properties of a dandelion that she could release with one little breath. I watched her uncover the treasure of an old Butterfinger wrapper under a bush, and then delighted in her bringing it to me as if it were a gift she made herself. I watched her walk up to a rather large bumblebee and say "Hi" and then walk away casually, completely unaware of the potential danger. And I watched her get dirty. Really dirty. I mean dirt-under-the-fingernails-that-I-just-painted dirty. And I watched her learn about this beautiful earth that God has created for us. I am so glad I slowed up today. I am so glad I took the time to watch my Sara discover God— even if she doesn't know that she did.

Personal Touch

Spend some time outside with your baby. Take a leisurely discovery walk on a beautiful day. The fresh air will do both of you some good. Take time to notice the sounds and scents and seasonal hues of God's amazing creation.

> *For since the creation of the world God's*
> *invisible qualities—his eternal power and*
> *divine nature—have been clearly seen,*
> *being understood from what has been made,*
> *so that men [and women and children]*
> *are without excuse.*
> —Romans 1:20

Prayer

Dear Father, instill in me a love of Your creation that I can, in turn, impart to my child. Help me to learn and to teach that You touch every part and detail of our lives and our world. Amen.

15

Lessons from the Yard

Show the wonder of your great love,
you who save by your right hand
those who take refuge in you.
                    —Psalm 17:7

*A*nother afternoon spent in the yard with Sara. I really felt God showing me insights today into just how human my daughter is. We have a nice-sized, fenced yard with endless exploration possibilities. But every once in a while, she will go up to the gate and get frustrated that I have closed it. I have closed it, of course, to keep her safe. But with all of the freedom she has to discover and run and play, it sometimes isn't enough for her. How human is that? Who of us hasn't rejoiced in the freedom that living in Christ affords us and, moments later, wished we could be somewhere else—like on the other side of the fence. We are given everything we could possibly want and more in our "yard," and we still look longingly over the fence, frustrated that we are so very confined. Oh, my human daughter.

But conversely, the freedom sometimes becomes *too much* for her. She will play contentedly for about an hour, and then she hits her breaking point. She becomes frustrated and irritable, and lets me know that she has had enough and wants to go in. And don't we all feel that way sometimes? We can feel overwhelmed by the possibilities and choices and just need a break. Sara seems to express, "Take me inside for a snack, Mommy. This is all too much right now." We, too, sometimes pray, "Take me inside, Abba Father, and hold me in Your arms for a while. Give me the boundaries that I act like I don't want. You know that deep inside I do. I am thankful that You give them to me when I am tired of this life."

A dog lives next door on the other side of our fence. Sara loves Gypsy. But I think she loves her so much because of the fence that separates them. She teases the dog just a little and has found that she is safe. When Gypsy barks, Sara laughs, but with a bit of fear on her face. Like Sara, we like to look at sin, we even like to play with it sometimes. But deep down, we know it is dangerous, and we are glad that God has placed a fence between it and us.

Sara has a plastic scooter, and I usually prop my feet on it while I read and she plays. But if she catches me doing it, she will stop her play and go out of her way to walk over and knock my feet off of it. Then she gets on it or pushes it around for a few seconds, giving the impression that she had planned to play with it all along. The truth is, she only wanted it because I had it. Again, how very human.

But being human has its vulnerable side, as well, such as when Sara needs what I like to call the "checking-in hug." She'll play for minutes at a time, then she'll walk over and cuddle with me for a few brief but cherished moments. It's as if she says, "I'm doing fine, just wanted to make sure you're still here and that you still love me." And don't we do that with God? We check in in the middle of our lives, stopping to get a hug and some reassurance from our ever-watchful heavenly Parent. "Just making sure You're still watching out for me, God. Just checking to see that You still love me."

I thought about my role in that yard today. How I was being the "God," so to speak, of our yard, making sure Sara didn't eat any bugs or fall on anything sharp. But the difference between me and God is that, in this instance, I was half-reading, half-watching Sara. I watched her when she was in my sight, but I didn't know what she was doing when she was behind me. I sometimes chose to turn around and look, and I sometimes chose to assume that she was doing fine. What a difference between God and me! God never reads on the job. He isn't too lazy to turn around to see what we are doing. And He is always watching—all of the time, no matter what.

Personal Touch

What is my point with all of this pondering? God speaks to us even in the littlest of things. So always be watching and listening for what He wants to share with you. Stop what you are doing right now and just study your little cherub(s). What are they up to?

> The LORD watches over you—
> the LORD is your shade at your right hand.
> —Psalm 121:5

Prayer

Dear Father, open my heart, mind, and eyes so I may see You in the details of my day. Help me feel Your Presence in my home, marriage, and mothering in a special way today. Amen.

16

For Sara, on the Arrival of Jack

Neither height nor depth, nor anything else in all creation,
will be able to separate us from the love of God that is in
Christ Jesus our Lord.

—Romans 8:39

You have lost part of me,
That much I expected.
But I lost part of you,
And I miss you.
I see you every day.
But now you glide past as if to say,
"I can go on, Mommy, with less of you."
But I can't.
I can't just go on.
Nothing has changed between us,

But everything has changed in our world.
My love has not changed,
But it can't be measured in time anymore.
Because moments are fewer.
And moments are rushed.
You glide past me again,
And I whisper, "I love you."
You push me away,
But you smile.
Because although something is missing,
And although something is lost now,
You know deeply, dear Sara, that my love remains.

Personal Touch

There are little moments of loss and gain in each of our lives every day. I had to give up being 100 percent available for Sara so that Jack could enter into our world. We have all adjusted beautifully, and I believe we have all come to love the new dynamics of our family of four, even more than when it was just the three of us. God brings us through situations that may not appear pleasant at the time but that bring rewards and joy we couldn't have predicted and wouldn't trade for the world.

Every good and perfect gift is from above,
coming down from the Father of the
heavenly lights, who does not change
like shifting shadows.
—James 1:17

Prayer

Dear Father, in my times of transition, I ask that You give me an eternal perspective so I may see what You see. Grant me the patience and strength to get to the other side with grace and creativity. And thank You for caring for me so much that you do not want me to stay in the same place forever. Amen.

17

Freeze Time

There is a time for everything,
and a season for every activity under heaven.
                    —Ecclesiastes 3:1

Part One

Can You freeze time?
Freeze these moments of so much love
That I don't know what to do with myself
Freeze these moments of so little sleep
That I don't remember my own name half the time
Freeze these moments of so much awe
That I can't help but praise Your Name for these amazing gifts
Freeze these moments of so many diapers
That I change more frequently than I change my own mind
Or do I—I can't decide?

Will You freeze time?
Because as it is, I can't see past tomorrow
My mind can't envision myself
As anything
Other than the mother of two under two
Who knew?
I wouldn't have believed it if someone had told me—
Five years and two kids ago
But why not?
What else could I possibly be doing?
This is my life
So please freeze time
Stop these moments from leaving
Keep the love, and the weariness, and the awe, and the diapers
Right here
For just a moment
Longer

Part Two

One day later . . .

I thought I could take my "two under two" to Target. My motive was pure. I wanted a few items of clothing—for me. (Heaven forbid!) I need something to wear. Something that would somehow fit my new body—the one that resembles a Dr. Seuss character. What was I thinking? After two attempts to enter the store—the first thwarted by whining and screaming children, the second because I was positive a clerk was about to call Child and Family Services—I left. I packed us back into the car and went home. Just like that. And they both screamed the entire way.

So, what was I was saying *just yesterday?* Something about *freezing time?* I've changed my mind. Please don't freeze it. Allow it to unfold at its normal pace. And I'll just keep a journal.

Personal Touch

Allow the pleasures of the moment to sink in—memorize your baby's face. Linger at the next feeding and look into each other's eyes. Freeze time in your mind because time moves so quickly, and these moments with your children will be like pictures you can revisit again and again. And it will be these snapshots that carry you through the more trying parenting times.

Prayer

Dear Father, impress upon my heart the wonder that is the creation of my baby. In the midst of the diapers and duties, help keep my focus on Jesus, Your love for me, and this gift. Amen.

18

Order My Days

But everything should be done in a fitting and orderly way.
*—*1 Corinthians 14:40

y daughter is twenty-two months old and my son is three months old. Most people react with, "Boy, you have your hands full!" My entire second pregnancy I thought, "What was I thinking? I can barely handle two when one is tucked safely inside my womb! How will I do this when they're both out in the world?" And I must admit, doubt hung over me like a dark cloud for the first two months of my son's life. I felt overwhelmed and helpless. I didn't think I'd be able to handle this for the long haul. But I've discovered something. Or maybe I should say *rediscovered?* I love being a mom! My kids are fabulous! My daughter is turning into a person right before my eyes. She is no longer just an extension of me—she is establishing her own vibrant identity. And my son is adorable. No longer an inanimate object, he now smiles when he hears my voice. I am enjoying myself and my children in a new way. I have somehow received rejuvenation in my calling as a stay-at-home mom. And I think it began when I started praying for God to come into my home to order my days, stretch my hours, and fill my minutes with His holiness. My priorities have changed. I stop doing the dishes to sit on the kitchen floor and play with my daughter. And I don't check the clock. I just play. And watch. Because God wants me to watch. He wants me to see that in the smallest details of my life, I can be blessed and loved by Him, in this case through my children.

So the next time your little ones tug on your leg, let the impatience drain away and allow them to tug on your heart. And enjoy. Truly, truly enjoy what God has given you.

Personal Touch

The more organized I become and the more routine my children's days are, the more time I have to focus on the important things—spending time with my kids; building my relationships with God, my husband, and my friends; working on my ministries. Try to have a daily plan, but wait expectantly for God's surprises.

For God is not a God of disorder but of peace.
—1 Corinthians 14:33

Prayer

Dear Father, come into my home and family. Show me how You want me to order my life and to spend my time. And show me how to revel in my precious baby and in the gift of this time in my life. Amen.

19

The Joy List

Are not my few days almost over?
Turn away from me so I can have a moment's joy.
—Job 10:20

All right. Pen in hand. Go.

Hitting all the green lights on the way to church, especially when we're running late. Finding a bargain on clothes. Parking spots close to the store. Dreaming big (and allowing myself to get excited). Jack sleeping until 7 A.M. Sara sleeping past 7 A.M. Writing a good article. Knowing what my gifts are. Knowing they come from God. Nursing Jack. The look Jack gets right after nursing. Sara's expanding vocabulary. Jack's coos and giggles. Photographs turning out really well. Not being too tired for . . . ! Finding the kitchen as clean in the morning as I left it the night before. Finding a card that says "Thank you for all you do" that my husband hid in the diaper bag. Books that speak my language and touch my heart. When I cook dinner and it's really good (not just "Beth" good). Long quiet-time opportunities.

"You've got mail!" People who extend help without expecting anything in return. Kevin taking Sara grocery shopping or to cut the grass. A few hours to run errands all by myself. The smell of a pretty candle. Songs that remind me of something wonderful—like a friend, God, love, mothering. A quiet car ride even when the kids are with me.

Stop.

Wow, there are a lot of good things in my life. Because God is good.

Personal Touch

You're having "one of those days"? Stop whatever you're doing. Find a piece of paper and a pen. Now write. Write down every thing in your life that brings you even a tad of joy—those little pleasant surprises that keep you going. Write for five minutes. Then read over the list. Maybe this will put a smile back on your face.

> *You have made known to me the path of life;*
> *you will fill me with joy in your presence,*
> *with eternal pleasures at your right hand.*
> —Psalm 16:11

Prayer

Dear Father, thank You for all the big and little gifts of joy that You give me each and every day. Make me more aware of what You're doing in my life. Amen.

20

Middle-of-the-Night Melody

He put a new song in my mouth.
—Psalm 40:3

At the time of this writing, my son is four months old. (By the time you read this, he will probably be graduating from junior high, but I digress.) Jack has been sleeping through the night for about two months with only occasional midnight showings. But for some reason, he was up last night. My first, and completely human, response was, "Please, Jesus, help him settle himself back to sleep." After a few minutes, I realized the little guy had no intention of tiring himself out any time soon. So I got up and nursed him. I really don't mind these nighttime feedings; I realize that Jack is probably my last child. So I like to savor these moments when I can. And it's moments like these that lead me to some of my most meaningful thoughts.

When my daughter was very young, I composed a chorus just for her:

Your mommy loves you, your mommy loves you,
Mommy loves Sara, your mommy loves you!

I didn't say it was Grammy-winning material. But it has become a little jingle that I sing several times a day to my precious girl and it always makes her smile. I've been thinking that it's only fair to write something for Jack. At 3:08 A.M., this is what I came up with:

You are my son and moon, You are my shining star,
I'm so glad God made you just who you are.
You are my son and moon, You are my precious boy,
·Can't imagine my life without you to enjoy.

Again, no one in Nashville is shaking in their boots, but it's pretty good in light of sleep deprivation.

It's these little things—the small gestures, the tiny thoughts—that will make lasting impressions on our children. They will remember that Mommy took the time to write a song just for them. And they will remember that Mommy broke out into horrible singing at the drop of a hat. And they will remember that Mommy loved to play with them.

Personal Touch

Today, stop and think of one little thing you can do for each of your children. Something special, something out of the ordinary. Surprise them. A few extra minutes to play in the tub. A piece of candy for behaving well all day. A video they get to see only on special occasions. Or just getting on the floor and playing with them, whatever they want to play.

> *His master replied, "Well done, good and*
> *faithful servant! You have been faithful with*
> *a few things; I will put you in charge of*
> *many things."*
> —Matthew 25:21

Prayer

Dear Father, help me realize how fleeting are these days. And help me to see that it will be the little things that my children remember. Please give me creativity to know how to touch my child's heart deeply with a memory that they may cherish for a lifetime. Amen.

21

Dear Jesus . . .

My soul thirsts for God, for the living God.
When can I go and meet with God?
—Psalm 42:2

Dear Jesus,

Both of the kids are whiny right now. It's as if they know what I'm trying to do. Sara is even blowing her nose into thin air because she knows I'll stop what I'm doing to clean her up. So my head is elsewhere, I must admit.

*O*h, how many of my journal entries sound like this! I'm so glad Jesus understands the plight of the woman, wife, mother, and homemaker. I am so glad that He is more interested in our heart's attitude than how many minutes we can squeeze in with Him. He is our amazing High Priest who has "been there, done that." He knows what we're going through each and every minute. The toilet clogging, the phone that won't stop ringing, the poop that was supposed to stay in the diaper, the child that never ceases crying. And he knows our internal struggles. The guilt that tugs at our hearts because we don't have enough time to "get it all done"—whatever "all" is. The guilt that says we're not giving our all to our kids. The guilt that reminds us that we haven't had a quiet time in two weeks. Jesus sees the messes—both external and internal. He knows how hard it is at this season of life. He wants to help us get through. And He wants us to depend on Him to do so.

I want to come near You, Jesus. Can I ask You to meet me more than halfway today? Amen.

Personal Touch

Don't be discouraged if you have only five minutes to spend with God each day. Please start with that. God is with you each and every day, all day. He created you for His pleasure. He wants a relationship with you. Take the time, any time that you can. He will be there when you come. And, yes, He will meet you more than halfway.

Then you will call upon me and come
and pray to me, and I will listen to you.
You will seek me and find me when you seek
me with all your heart.
—Jeremiah 29:12–13

Prayer

Dear Father, thank You for wanting to spend time with me. Increase my faith so that I believe that truth and believe it so deeply that I can't help but want to spend time with You, too. But I ask that You quiet my heart. Clear out the murkiness of thinking and the chaos of mothering that steers my life, and bring rejuvenation, patience, and love into my vision. Amen.

22

Sole Provider

Put their hope in God, who richly provides us
with everything for our enjoyment.
—1 Timothy 6:17

I was playing with my four-month-old son today. I had
him sitting in my lap, lifting up his arms, tickling him,
making faces. Anything to get him to giggle and break out
into that fabulous smile God gave him. And I began to cry.
At that moment I had so much love for him, it overflowed
my heart and spilled out. And I said to him, "Do you have
any idea how much Mommy loves you, Jack?" And he said
to me (this is where you need to use your imagination),
"Mommy, you have no idea what love is. You may love me
unconditionally. But right now, at this moment in time, I
love you solely. You have Daddy and Sara and God and
friends in your life. But for right now, I have only you. You
are my world."

I'm not being prideful or immodest when I say that.
During these first few months, we moms are our babies'

everything. I don't kid myself that this lasts longer than maybe five or six months. But for right now, I am *it* to him. I am Jack's best thing. What a privilege. What an honor. What a responsibility! I am the one to show him all that is good and perfect and right at this moment in time. And that is not the kind of thing I want to take lightly.

Personal Touch

If you have a baby, take a few moments and let the thought sink in—today you are his or her sole provider. Don't let it overwhelm you, instead be grateful for the blessing. Now take a moment to consider what this means to you spiritually. God wants and desires to be your sole/soul Provider. Are you letting Him? What steps can you take today to offer yourself to Him and relinquish control?

I said to the LORD, "You are my Lord;
apart from you I have no good thing."
—Psalm 16:2

Prayer

Dear Father, thank You for babies. Thank You for their amazing dependence upon us that bonds them to us for a lifetime. Help me see today as one step in this process of forming my relationships on solid ground—my relationship with my child and my relationship with You. Amen.

23

Daddy's Girl

Honor your father and your mother,
*as the L*ORD *your God has commanded you, so that you*
may live long and that it may go well with you in the
*land the L*ORD *your God is giving you.*

—Deuteronomy 5:16

At church today I caught a glimpse of an amazing father-daughter relationship. I was intrigued and challenged and given hope all in that one moment. What did I see that touched me so deeply?

After our congregation sang a chorus, we did the usual "greeting of those around you." I watched a father greet his fifteen-year-old daughter. What's the big deal? For one thing, girls of that age tend to be embarrassed by their fathers. That she even acknowledged him is amazing enough. What struck me, though, was how they addressed each other. Their fondness for one another and the way they were comfortable with each other was foreign to me. They did a handshake kind of thing. It was so brief that I have difficulty explaining it. But the daughter was not embarrassed by her father. She didn't simply acknowledge him, she greeted him warmly and affectionately. The handshake lingered a moment. Long enough for me to zoom thirteen or so years into the future and picture my Sara embracing her father in public without shame.

Why did this hit me so hard? Maybe because what you see in public is an accurate reflection of what is being built in private.

Personal Touch

Talk to your husband today about one thing each of you can do with your child that will build on the parent-child relationship to insure its strength in the future. And then each of you make a plan to spend some alone time with each of your children. What an impact this will make on their little hearts!

> *"So there is hope for your future,"*
> *declares the LORD.*
> *"Your children will return to their own land."*
> —Jeremiah 31:17

Prayer

Dear Father, I ask not only that my husband and I build something special and unique and strong with our children, but that we both build something in private with You, our God. And may our relationships with You keep us from being publicly ashamed and unable to acknowledge You as our Father. Amen.

24

Whom Do They See?

Follow my example, as I follow the example of Christ.
—1 Corinthians 11:1

I should be able to say to my husband and children, "You want to see a godly woman? Look at me. You want to know what Christ is like? Watch me."

Tall order. Can my husband say that about me? He sees me at my worst. But even through my most awful, can he still find Jesus underneath the mess? I would like to think he can—sometimes, at least. And though Kevin sees the bad and ugly, my kids see me *constantly*. All day long, every day. They see me start the day in a bad mood. They see me drop something on the floor and say, "Ahh, nuts!" (I know, it could be worse, but now my daughter drops things just so she can say "Ahh, nuts!") They hear me call my fellow drivers "morons." They see my impatience when there is yet another price check. And you call *this* the express lane?! They see me screen my calls when I don't want to handle another conversation.

But I hope that they see more than that. I hope they see me have my quiet time each day (well, almost each day). I hope they see me smile when talking to their daddy on the phone. I hope they see me get excited over a ministry project or something that uses my talents. I hope they see me trying to take care of household duties. I hope they see me stop to play with them. I hope they see me create an atmosphere of open praise and prayer in our home.

In other words, I know these people sometimes see the worst in me. But I hope that, at times, they can see *past* me to see Jesus *in* me.

Personal Touch

Let's work on being attentive—Jesus would have been. He probably would have been fairly neat in appearance, on time for appointments, and considerate with details and in relationships. Your family, the people closest to you, have been given specifically to you, to minister to first and foremost. They deserve the best of you that you can give.

> *Her children arise and call her blessed;*
> *her husband also, and he praises her.*
> —Proverbs 31:28

Prayer

Dear Father, may Your Spirit remind me each day to show Jesus to my children. Because if I do not, who will? Amen.

25

Looming Monotony and Oatmeal . . . Again

Meanwhile we groan, longing to be clothed
with our heavenly dwelling.
—2 Corinthians 5:2

It's 7:37 A.M. Let me rephrase that. It's *only* 7:37 A.M. I've been up for over an hour and a half. Seems like three days. Sara is shunning her oatmeal, and Jack is already whining (with an hour to go before nap time). Monotony stretches before me, and I feel overwhelmed by the prospect of another day.

I'm not having a bad day, per se. It's just . . . it's just *another* day. Another day on the way to being just like yesterday and probably very similar to tomorrow. Do you ever feel like this?

I have already breathed a prayer to Jesus, "Please come be with me. I need Your help." Yet, I feel the same. Sometimes my prayers seem to hit the ceiling and just kind of float there. I know Jesus is with me and that He is helping me, but I don't always *feel* it.

So what can I do about this? I don't have all the answers. Far from it. There are some days I just feel like sighing, and for no real reason at all.

I have one blessing that I'm sure of, though, one thing that helps me if I allow it to sink into my soul: if I am a believer, then I have everything in the world to be happy about. My sins are forgiven and I'm going to heaven. What else is there? Everything else in life is just details.

Unfortunately, it's the details that I am struggling with this morning. And that's fine. No one ever said life would be easy. It is normal for us to yearn for more. Just as long as we yearn while allowing the peace of God to comfort us.

Well, look at that? It's *already* 8:12 A.M. My, how time flies. See, it's all in the way you look at it.

Personal Touch

Don't be too hard on yourself if you're having a "sigh" day. Even if it's for no apparent reason. We are human. But let us be thankful that we have the power of God to help us overcome these attitudes of discontentment, restlessness, and boredom.

> *Let us not become weary in doing good, for at*
> *the proper time we will reap a harvest if we do*
> *not give up.*
> —Galatians 6:9

Prayer

Dear Father, I ask right now, as I feel so ho-hum, that You will touch my heart in an amazing way. Help me to feel Your love for me so I may rise above this monotony. Please meet me where I am. Amen.

26

Do You Work?

*Whatever you do, work at it with all your heart, as working
for the Lord, not for men, since you know you will receive
an inheritance from the Lord as a reward. It is the
Lord Christ you are serving.*
—Colossians 3:23–24

"Do you work?" Panic set in. I checked through all the
answers in my brain. Do I work? I composed myself and
then said, "Yes, I do work. I'm a full-time mom." Why
does that question still make me freak out? Do I work? I
work harder than you do, sir, 24/7, 365 days a year. By no
means am I complaining. And I'm certainly not trying to
compare.

It's interesting, though. After answering, "Yes, I'm a full-
time mom," I often see a vacant look in the eyes of the
questioner. I've been thinking about this question because,
obviously, I'm a stay-at-home mom. I'm writing a book for
mothers of young children—not all of whom will be stay-
at-home moms. But after some time, I've finally resolved

my own feelings of being "just a mom." (And if I hear me describe myself that way one more time, I'm going to scream.) The problem is, I don't really feel like I'm *just a mom*—until someone asks me if I work. I suppose I could politely correct the next person by saying, "If you're wondering if I work *outside* the home, no. My work is *inside* the home."

Or—what a shame I didn't think of this sooner—"Yes, I do work. I'm in management. I specialize in training." I can't wait to try that one.

Personal Touch

Don't be discouraged if some people don't understand your God-given role. Remember, if you are a believer, you are in full-time ministry. If you are a mother, you have a more-than-full-time job. Never, ever forget those truths.

> *Now we ask you, brothers, to respect those*
> *who work hard among you.*
> —1 Thessalonians 5:12

Prayer

Dear Father, please instill in me a healthy pride for my vocation as a mother. Whether I stay at home or not, mothering is my priority, and I ask that You remind me of that commitment today. And I ask that You help me to be the kind of woman who can gracefully and creatively embrace my calling as a mom. Amen.

27

Brotherly and Sisterly Love

Be devoted to one another in brotherly love.
Honor one another above yourselves.
— Romans 12:10

When I was pregnant with Jack, but didn't yet know he was a boy, I attended a Hearts-at-Home conference. That weekend God brought a gift to me that—though I didn't know it at the time—will forever be a part of the Corcoran family tradition.

Part of me, you see, was hoping for another girl. I told myself that I wanted a sister for Sara—something I hadn't had. I just liked the idea of two little girls. For some reason, though, I had a feeling that Jack was a Jack. We even began calling him "Baby Jack" a few months before he came along. I needed a change of heart, however, and I was praying for it. Fortunately, God heard and answered my prayers.

At the Hearts-at-Home conference, the guest singers were Steve and Annie Chapman and their college-aged son and daughter. These two young adults sang what is called the "Brother-Sister Song." When the boy was ten and the sister was turning eight, he wrote a poem for her birthday. The poem was later turned into a song, which these two young people sang to each other:

Here's to my sister, remember every day . . .
No matter what I've said, here's what I'd like to say,
I will always love you, be with you 'til the end,
When no one else is around, I will be your friend.
'Cause I love my sister, and I always will.
I'm proud to be your brother, that's how I feel.
Someday when we're far away and the miles keep us apart,
I'm gonna whisper, "I love my sister,"
And you'll know it in your heart.

Here's to my brother, remember every day . . .
No matter what I've said, here's what I'd like to say,
I will always love you, be with you 'til the end,
When no one else is around, I will be your friend.
'Cause I love my brother, and I always will.
I'm proud to be your sister, that's how I feel.
Someday when we're far away and the miles keep us apart,
You will discover, "I love my brother,"
And you'll know it in your heart.

Someday when we're far away and the miles keep us apart,
I'm gonna whisper, "I love my sister,"
You will discover, "I love my brother,"
And we'll know it in our hearts.[1]

I tucked that song into the back of my head, the months went by, and Jack came along—my precious Jack. And in the midst of getting back on my feet and in the groove of being a mother of two, I remembered that song and tracked it down. I play it almost every day. Sara may not have the sister that I wanted her to have. But I would like to believe that I gave birth to one of her best friends. And I want to do everything I can to insure that.

> *I'm gonna whisper, "I love my sister,"*
> *You will discover, "I love my brother,"*
> *And we'll know it in our hearts.*

Personal Touch

If you are the mother of more than one child, it is largely your responsibility to nurture that special bond between siblings. I urge you to creatively foster and encourage that relationship today. If you are the mother of one, consider enrolling your child in a play group or preschool program so he or she may begin learning new relational skills.

> *Your [children] will be taught by the Lord,*
> *and great will be your children's peace.*
> —Isaiah 54:13

Prayer

Dear Father, thank You for the different personalities and genders in my precious, little family. Help me to see that You have ordained all of us to be together for this season of time. Work in my heart to help me create an atmosphere where we can learn and grow in our love for each other. Amen.

28

Tea Set or Chemistry Set?

Yet, O LORD, you are our Father.
We are the clay, you are the potter;
we are all the work of your hand.
—Isaiah 64:8

*W*hile watching television yesterday a commercial grabbed my attention. The woman claimed, "Taking chemistry class led me to a life of crime. I am an investigator for murders, rapes, and robberies." She said that what she learned in chemistry class gave her the foundation for a challenging career that she loved. I was right with her up to that point. "You go, girl," I thought, because I believe in the equality of man and woman in the eyes of God, and I have every intention of providing opportunities for Sara and for Jack that are equally challenging.

But then she said, "So instead of giving your daughter a tea set, give her a chemistry set."

"What did she just say?" I was appalled. *"Instead of?!"* This commercial, sponsored by the Women's College Coalition, touted the slogan, "Give a girl the best and that is what she will become."

I grew up believing I could do anything I wanted with my life. I went to college and began work on a Master's degree. But my chosen career, at least for now, is to be a wife, mother, and homemaker. What higher calling is there on earth? I might have loved a chemistry set—if science were my forte—and I'm sure it would have served me well to learn those skills. But I also would have loved a tea set. I would have loved to discover the art of hospitality, cooking, manners, and friendship-building at a young age.

So, Hollywood and society-at-large, please stop knocking the women of the world—intelligent and creative women—who are choosing the career of mothering and homemaking. What we are building in our homes has far more significance than what can be explained with a microscope and some goggles. And change your "instead of" to "in addition to." I am sure most children—girls *and* boys—would benefit from both a chemistry set *and* a tea set. Just as our world benefits from both scientists and mothers.

Personal Touch

Plan one way you can instill in your child the often-missed concept of living abundantly now with the lives God has given them. Open up options to them so they know that, with God's leading, there is nothing they cannot do.

In everything set them an example by
doing what is good.
—Titus 2:7

Prayer

Dear Father, I lift up my children and the amazing abilities You have wired into them. I ask that You will help me pinpoint their gifts and personalities at an early age so I can best aid You in molding them into Your intended creations. Amen.

29

Am I Done?

Therefore, a [woman] cannot discover
anything about [her] future.
                    —Ecclesiastes 7:14

"You have a girl and a boy? Are you two done?" My son is five months old. I already miss having a newborn around the house and the awe that accompanies one. I was very blessed with wonderful pregnancies and amazing births. I would do it all again in an instant. Am I done? I am blessed to have the choice, as opposed to life making the choice for me. Yet, I have no idea. Right now, I am fifty/fifty on the issue. I love pregnancy and delivery. I would love for Sara to have a sister. I love babies. I love being a mom.

But who's to say the next pregnancy and delivery would be as wonderful as my last two? And there is no pill that guarantees a sister. And babies grow up. And I am already a mom. And my son hasn't even begun to crawl, eat, or talk yet. So check back with me in about six months. My husband claims he is done. "We have one of each," he says. "What other combination is there?" In fact, I had to do some convincing to even try for baby Jack. So in light of our oneness, if Kevin is done having children, then I am done having children.

So far, two children are manageable. I can still have a life outside of my home, work at ministry, use my gifts, and still keep most of my sanity intact. With two, I can (I hope) love each of them well. I will likely not feel stretched beyond what I am able to give.

So as of this moment, "Yes, I'm done." Then again, no one but God knows what is in store for me. Possibly a little surprise, another new combination of genes that only God could dream up.

Personal Touch

Are you struggling with the "is my family complete" blues? This is a tough one. Will you be content to hold only the babies of friends from now on? Or do you feel that you have the love, energy, time, and the resources to give to another little one? Bring your desires and concerns to your husband and to your Father.

> *Since no [one] knows the future,*
> *who can tell [her] what is to come?*
> —Ecclesiastes 8:7

Prayer

Dear Father, thank You for placing within me the desire to have children. When it comes to the completion of my family, please work in my heart and through my circumstances to help me make the best choices for myself, my marriage, and my relationship with You. Amen.

Author's Note

Dear baby whom I'll never conceive,

I've been thinking a lot about you lately. Perhaps I need to say good-bye. I know you have never existed. I know I haven't had you and lost you. But I can almost picture you in my mind's eye. Not the physical features—I can't even imagine if you would have been my son or daughter. I just know that I will never meet you. You will never be a part of our family. I will never carry you inside me. Or hold you in my arms. Or kiss your sweet cheeks. Or watch your first step. Or hear your first words. Or hold your hand. Or teach you to ride a bike. Or read a story to you. Or pass on my love for writing to you. Or talk to you about Jesus. Or send you off to school. Or hold you during your first broken heart. Or let you go. No, that's not true. I have to let you go now. Before I even have you. Before God even creates you. I would have loved you. Maybe not well—maybe not as well as you would have needed. And maybe that's why you won't be coming to be with me. But I miss you. I will miss you all of my days. And I will always wonder in the back of my mind what you would have been like.

Good-bye, Baby.
Momma

30

Friends . . . Who Needs 'Em?

Two are better than one,
because they have a good return for their work:
If one falls down,
[her] friend can help [her] up.
But pity the [woman] who falls
and has no one to help [her] up!
                    —Ecclesiastes 4:9–10

I could name over twenty women whom I respect and would love to befriend. I'd like to share in their unique journeys, in hopes of emulating their Christian walk as women, wives, and mothers. But I don't have time to cultivate twenty close friendships.

A couple of years ago, a friend and I began a women's ministry at our church. We wanted to foster friendships during this busy season of our lives. I have found it to be an amazing ministry, and I've come to know many women better. But I still feel disconnected sometimes. A quick phone call here and there, a note of encouragement dropped in the mail or one received with a thankful heart, a chat between a church service and grabbing the kids out of child care on a Sunday. Those moments add up to build beautiful friendships, but they aren't always enough for us to really get to know each other.

Lately I've been feeling lonely, despite being in a rich season friendship-wise. When it comes to quantity, I've never been less lacking for companionship. My dilemma is, I long for depth, not abundance.

Jesus chose twelve men to invest in, three that were very close and, of those, one referred to as the "one Jesus loved." Only twelve to closely focus on. What better model than Christ Himself? I have spent some time in prayer and thought and have made my own list. (Mine has only ten— but I'm not Jesus!) It includes a variety of wonderful women who don't even know they are on my "list." Don't misunderstand, I will not forbid myself to befriend someone just because she's not on my "list." I feel, though, that God has placed particular women in my life for specific reasons, either to minister to, be ministered by, or both. A couple are women that I will be pouring a lot into, receiving only eternal rewards if I have been able to encourage them. And others will be blessing me left and right, just by being in my life.

This list of mine is refreshing. It lifts the burden of having to be everything to everybody, especially as I am in a place of leadership right now. I will devote myself to prayer and encouragement and getting to know these women in the next year. I look forward to the results, both now and ever after.

Personal Touch

If you are blessed with many friends and have no struggles in this area, I encourage you to step up your affirmations to them. Don't allow yourself to take your friendships for granted. If you are struggling in this area, I strongly urge you to spend time in prayer, handing over your cares to the God who is waiting to comfort and help you.

Also, if two lie down together, they will keep warm.
But how can one keep warm alone?
Though one may be overpowered,
two can defend themselves.
A cord of three strands is not quickly broken.
—Ecclesiastes 4:11–12

Prayer

Dear Father, I first want to praise You for being the ultimate Friend and an amazing example to follow. I also want to thank You for each woman that is in my life. I pray that I can view them through Your eyes, as gifts from You, here to teach me the lessons that You want me to learn, here for me to be Your hands and Your feet as You show me how to minister love to each of them. Show me how to love them well and love them much. You know my heart better than anyone. If I'm struggling to develop friendship, I ask that You heal the pain and bring someone special into my life. Thank You for the precious gift of friendship. Amen.

31

A Look Inside
My Journal

*"For my thoughts are not your thoughts,
neither are your ways my ways,"
declares the LORD.*

—Isaiah 55:8

Random Day 1

My best friend is going on a missions trip to India next month. She e-mailed me with a long and detailed list of prayer requests. That got me thinking. Yes, going to a foreign land to share the gospel is major kingdom work. But why does that require *more* faith, *more* obedience, *more* prayer, and *more* dependence than her "regular" life—or mine? Her life intersects with lost souls in the workplace each day. My life is bound with two eager little hearts listening and watching my every word and deed and move. Talk about needing faith, obedience, prayer, and dependence. We need those elements in our "normal" lives each day. Please give me a "missions trip" excitement and mindset on where I'm at right now—wife, mom, friend, writer, and "minister."

Random Day 2

I have completely let my quiet time go. Rather than a time I desire and protect, it's beginning to feel like another obligation to check off my to-do list. Please reveal any hidden sin or wrong thinking or impure motive that, in my humanness, I cannot see. Help me become holy. I need to start small so I may see the progress clearly and not feel discouraged or abandoned by You. So I ask that today I choose the high road in just one incident. Help me, just once, to be clearly unselfish, patient, and loving.

Random Day 3

I thank You, Father, for the spiritual blessings of salvation and thirteen years of being Your child. I thank You for open access to You, Your provisions, and Your power. I thank You for the personal blessings of Sara and Jack (better than my dreams!), a wonderful and selfless husband, amazing friends, and ministries that allow me to stretch and grow. Thank You for my life and all its goodness and all its imperfections.

Random Day 4

I confess that my mind is elsewhere. I wonder if first-thing-in-the-morning quiet times are not for me. Please guide me in this area. I want to think of the best time to spend with You each day.

[In taking an idea from Bill Hybels's *Too Busy Not to*

Pray, I began writing about my "yesterday" and all its bless-ings, both practical and spiritual.][1] Yesterday was Monday. A busy at-home day, as it usually is. Odds and ends to catch up on, the house, laundry, "projects" Kevin asked me to do. That is my typical Monday. Unfortunately, I don't remember much about my actual Monday. (How sad is that?) Let me think: I got my first spontaneous "I love you, Mommy" from Sara. I read three chapters of *Too Busy Not to Pray.* I actually made dinner. Kevin and I did devotions together. Jack sat in the highchair and ate Cheerios by him-self for the first time. It was a gorgeous day weather-wise, so I sat on the porch and had my quiet time while the kids napped. All in all a good day. Did You think so?

Random Day 5

The other day, a girlfriend asked me, "If you could do anything in the world right now, what would it be?" I in-stantly said, "Get my book published!" Her question stuck with me, however, and I expanded on it. I asked myself the following questions and presented them to God: (1) If I could *do* anything at this time in my life, what would it be? (2) If I could *have* anything at this time in my life, what would it be? (3) If I could *be* anything at this time in my life, what would it be? I answered these for myself and then prayed, wondering if God were the one to lay these dreams on my heart. I am waiting in "passionate expecta-tion" for His answers.

Personal Touch

Keeping a journal can be one of your best tools for growth. Being able to track God's hand in your life will keep you going in the dark times and will build your faith as you watch Him write your life's story.

> *You show that you are a letter from*
> *Christ, . . . written not with ink but with the*
> *Spirit of the living God, not on tablets of stone*
> *but on tablets of human hearts.*
> —2 Corinthians 3:3

Prayer

Dear Father, as I spend time writing down my thoughts— writing letters to You—I ask that You meet me there. I ask that You speak clearly to me and show me Your movement in my life. Amen.

32

Juggling Act

*A truly good wife is the most precious treasure a man
   can find!*
Her husband depends on her, and she never lets him down. . . .
With her own hands she gladly makes clothes. . . .
She gets up before daylight to prepare food for her family. . . .
She knows how to buy land and how to plant a vineyard. . . .
She stays busy until late at night.
          —Proverbs 31:10–11, 13, 15, 16, 18 CEV

I've had an interesting couple of weeks. Let me give you
an idea. But I preface this by quoting from *Ally McBeal*, a
popular TV show. Ally tends to focus on herself, *a lot*, and
a friend asked, "Ally, what makes *your* problems so much
bigger than everybody else's?" And she said, "Because
they're *mine*." I didn't draw up this list, though, out of
complete self-absorption. I wanted to show you what may
be on the mind of one typical woman.

In the past few weeks I've had the following to think
about (in no particular order): a friend is coming for the

weekend; I attended a thought-provoking women's retreat last month; I'm in a small group that started up a few weeks ago; our Women's Ministries Spring Celebration takes place in a couple of weeks; my grandma recently found out she has cancer; Sara, now almost three, has been referred for an evaluation for a potential speech delay, and our new insurance may not cover the therapy; I've been asked to give the Mother's Day talk at church; my son's first birthday party is next month; our family needs to plan for the summer when my husband Kevin is off from work because he's a teacher; a friend and her baby are coming for a visit; my son's first two teeth are *taking a month to arrive!* And for the past three weeks, I haven't been feeling well. I recently found out there might be something wrong with my liver. But there was a mix-up at the lab, and instead of finding out my results last Friday, I won't know anything until tomorrow. (Author's note: Turned out, I ended up walking around with mononucleosis, and I didn't even know until it was gone!)

That list didn't even include the thoughts that daily run through my head on autopilot: laundry—there's always laundry; trying to cook on a *somewhat* regular basis; diapers, diapers, and more diapers. Will this house ever be really clean? Do I *really* care? Did I mention diapers? Am I going to make time for my "Experiencing God" lesson today or will Rosie O'Donnell win out? Am I going to make time for Tae-Bo today or will a nap sound better? If one more telemarketer calls for Mrs. "COCK-ran" today, I'm going to rip the cord out of the wall. And the phone—one morning this week it began ringing at 6:59 A.M. By 9:30 A.M., I had received and made thirteen phone calls. I feel like I'm running a business!

Then there are the bigger things always on my mind: Am I telling Sara and Jack all I need to about Jesus? Am I loving Sara specifically the way Sara needs to be loved, and Jack specifically the way Jack needs to be loved? Do I put their needs before mine? I'm home with my children all day, every day, but am I spending *quality* time with them and not just *quantity?* Do my kids feel taken care of? Do they know that they come before a phone call, housework, friends, ministry, and so forth? (As I say this, I'm recalling throwing animal crackers at Sara while I was on the phone, trying to stop her from saying, "Mommy, mommy, mommy, mommy, mommy . . .")

I feel very busy sometimes. But am I just busy doing busywork? Or am I busy doing things that will last for eternity? Am I taking care of my home in such a way that guests could stop by any time and I wouldn't freak out? In my busyness do I live in my home as if Jesus were there right beside me? Am I loving my husband on a consistent, selfless basis? Are his needs placed before my own? Are his needs placed before the kids'? Does he know that he is the most important person in my life? Am I making him the most important person in my life? Do my friends feel loved and encouraged? Am I involved enough at church? Am I *too* involved? Am I spending enough time with God so that He is able to change me?

On a daily basis my life does not *feel* as overwhelming as it may sound. Yes, I've got a lot going on. But I'm not trying to bring attention to all *I* do. My point is that I bet your mom or your wife or you, the woman of your home, balances a list of concerns very similar to mine. A wonderful book, *The Power of a Praying Wife* by Stormie Omartian, says that women are the hearts of the home. Single or married, mom or not, women have been given the responsibility by God to set the tone for our surroundings. It is a wonderful and creative privilege but also a huge task. We have a lot on our minds. And we have a lot that we need to give to Jesus.

Personal Touch

Okay, the Proverbs 31 woman seems a bit out of your league, huh? Don't despair. Here are a couple of theories that I like to cling to when I find myself in the comparison game with Mrs. P31. This narrative describes a woman's complete life, not one particular season in time; or better yet, this is a compilation of characteristics of godly women (plural!). Take a deep breath, you're not in this race to beat anyone, just to love your God and your family as well as you can with His help.

> *She is strong and graceful, as well as cheerful about the future. . . .*
> *A woman who honors the Lord deserves to be praised.*
> —Proverbs 31:25, 30 CEV

Prayer

Dear Father, I so desperately want to be all that I can be for You, but it can feel so overwhelming sometimes. There is always so much that has to be done, so much I want to do, so much I know I should do. Please empower me to be the best me—the me You had in mind when You created me. Amen.

33

Behind the Mask

On the outside you appear to people as righteous but on the inside you are full of hypocrisy.

—Matthew 23:28

t our women's retreat a couple of weeks ago, our speaker talked about our *person* and our *personage*. Our person is who we really are when no one is looking. Our personage is who the world sees. Since then, I've felt convicted to work on blending those two images of myself. I want the who I am in private to look more like the who I am in public, and vice versa. Over the past year I've heard two comments about me that really stuck with me. Last year I attended a Hearts-at-Home conference for stay-at-home moms. I told a friend that I had attended a seminar entitled "The Effects of Prayerlessness." She said, "I'm surprised you thought you needed that." For some reason, she didn't think that prayer was something that *I* struggled with. Then another friend at church said she was glad she got to know me better through a small group we both attend. She thought I had it all together until she learned I didn't cook. Now, I don't think she actually believed I was problem-free and sinless until she found out about the cooking. But I do think there is a lesson to be learned from her statement: In our society, even in our churches, most of us put our best selves forward, not wanting people to see who we really are. Because then we'd be found out for the *hypocrites* we really are. Everybody knows that no one has everything together, but I think we sometimes gaze longingly into other people's lives and think, "What if?" or "If only I had her life, then I could . . ."

Most women judge each other and themselves a little harshly. We forget that God created each of us uniquely and lovingly and for a specific purpose.

I have been a follower of Christ for over thirteen years. I am surrounded by people and a Lord who love me. But there is more to me than the personage I bring to church or walk around with in public. The real me, the person beneath the personage, looks more like this: I have a place for scotch tape in my house, and I know right where it is. I even carry some in my purse for "tape emergencies." But don't open up my Tupperware cabinet at home because you'd be pelted by a shower of plastic! I have wonderful friendships, but I sometimes feel very lonely and on my own. I love to write and occasionally receive a compliment, here and there, but I wrote a book of devotion for young moms over a year ago and can't get an agent or a publisher. (Author's note: Mission accomplished.) My marriage is not where my husband and I would like it to be. I love, absolutely *love*, to colead and co-organize the women's ministries, but the reason for starting the moms' group two years ago with my partner was not completely selfless. One day two women were standing next to me talking about starting a play group and who they should invite, and they completely ignored me. So in my hurt and sadness and tears, I wanted to start something where all women would feel welcome. I am so thankful for the close relationship between my husband and our daughter. But I picture myself trying to control it as the years go by to help insure they stay close.

All of this to say two things. One, *I need Jesus*. Life can be so hard. I cannot love my husband, my kids, my family, and my friends without Jesus showing me how. And two, from Galatians 6:3–5: "Make a careful exploration of who *you* are and the work *you* have been given, and then sink yourself into that. *Don't be impressed with yourself. Don't compare yourself with others*. Each of you must take responsibility for doing the creative best you can with your own life" (*The Message*, italics added).

We all—women and men—need to stop looking around and comparing ourselves to others. The grass is *not* greener on the other side; it's just a different shade. We need to pray for a happy medium, the peace that falls somewhere between puffing ourselves up and knocking ourselves down. We all get hit by stuff in this life. We all have good points and bad points. And we all are sinners in need of a Savior. I cannot be a wife without His help, and I can't be a mom without His wisdom. It's been said, "I am less important than I think I am, but more important than I'll ever know."

Personal Touch

I encourage and challenge you to take a step today to blend your personage and your person. It is in our authenticity and true sharing that we can support and help each other.

> *Each one should test [her] own actions. Then*
> *[she] can take pride in [herself], without*
> *comparing [herself] to somebody else.*
> —Galatians 6:4

Prayer

Dear Father, as I see myself for who I really am, I know I have a long way to go before my personal and public selves begin to line up. Please point out areas where I am not publicly being the "real me," and then strengthen me to take steps to live more authentically. Amen.

34

View from the Mountaintop

Let the people of Sela sing for joy;
let them shout from the mountaintops.
                                    —Isaiah 42:11

I have been there. In fact, I just spent four glorious months at the top of my magnificent mountain. However, I'm currently on the journey down.

I am a woman and, therefore, am emotional—most of the time. But I made a decision that one aspect of my life will not be driven by my feelings. That area is my spiritual walk. It's true that just the thought of what Jesus did for me on the cross can bring tears to my eyes. And His miracles in my life through my children can also get me choked up. I can and do get emotional about God's hand in my life.

By spiritual walk I'm talking about my daily journey. If I were to base my walk on my feelings day-to-day, I would have a quiet time maybe every two weeks. I would worship only after having a fabulous day with my kids. I would attend church only after a solid and long night's sleep. I would serve others only . . . well, you get the picture. I do not wait for the feelings to kick in before I make the move toward growth. In fact, a good portion of my personal experience with Christ has, on my end, been a deliberate choice rather than spontaneous inspiration. And I don't think that's wrong. I think I must move along the spiritual path regardless of my thoughts or my mind-set from moment to moment.

Having said all that, let me tell you about my mountaintop experience. Driven and fostered almost entirely by a divine sensation that I cannot express, I felt it wrap around my every waking moment when I was in it, and I feel its absence now that it is gone. My encounter lasted for about four months. I am the first to admit that we must be careful not to measure our faith through experience alone. However, I was able to sit back and watch God move in my life in a mighty way. I saw the work He did. I believe He brought me up the mountain to accomplish several things, all with one purpose—to raise the standard of my obedience.

He began by asking me to do some public speaking. I'd rather have oral surgery without anesthesia than speak in public, but I not only did it, I got a rush from it. Go figure. Father knows best.

He then asked me to initiate restoration and refreshment in a relationship that had been moving along a path of mediocrity. My self-absorption had kept me from taking these steps before this moment. But I could no longer deny His voice. This particular relationship began to flourish on that mountain. Hmm . . . He knows what He's talking about.

Another relationship needed healing. In fact, in a Bible study I was doing with a friend, one session was titled

"Fixing Broken Relationships." It might well have said, "Fixing Broken Relationships, Beth." OK, God, I hear You. I vowed not to enter His Presence again until I took a step of reconciliation. Another clean slate. Another huge stride. Peace at heart is a precious thing. How did You know, Father, that I'd feel so incredibly unburdened?

Then regarding ministry, He said to me, "Let go." By this point, my faith in His care for me was so built up, it didn't cross my mind to reply with anything other than, "Yes, Daddy." Sweet relief, sweet freedom. In letting go, I can serve more fully. In letting go, I can live out my giftedness even more wholly. And in letting go, I can open up ministry opportunities for other women. His ways are higher than my ways, but I've taken one step closer to understanding His ways. I tip my hat to You, God. You know me better than I know myself.

Oswald Chambers said, "Our faith must be built on strong, determined confidence in Him." May I add—and nothing else. He brought me up the mountain to teach me His truth and to strengthen my faith, but mostly to change me.

As desperately as I desire to stay "up there" on my mountaintop, I understand that I cannot. Life is lived out daily, down here in the valley. In fact, we are created for the valleys. The peaks are for inspiration. I must take what God changed in me and use it. I must do everything in my power, with the enabling of the Spirit, to live with a higher level of obedience to Him. He has the right to call me to do anything that He desires and sees fit. And I must do whatever He asks. That is what was shaped into me during the past few months. That's what God says to do. He says it because He is God. And He does know best.

In the meantime, however, I struggle with this loss. I miss the ease in which I walked and talked with God as did Eve, my heart imagines, in the garden. I miss the ever-present desire for more of Him, for the feeling that I was in His presence at all times. But I must go on, I must pray for the depth and strength of character to "do the next thing," even though the feelings have faded.

Personal Touch

Have you ever had a mountaintop season in your life with God? If you have, don't dwell on wishing that you could "go back" to that time. Life is filled with both experiences—the mountaintop times to teach us and the valley times to live out what we've learned. Think back to one of the mountain times and try to remember how you felt. Jot down what made it "different" from other seasons in your faith walk.

> *Come, let us go up to the mountain of the LORD,*
> *to the house of the God of Jacob.*
> *He will teach us his ways,*
> *so that we may walk in his paths.*
> —Micah 4:2

Prayer

Dear Father, thank You for those extended times of peace and closeness that You have brought to my life. I want to go back, but I know that it is only in Your time and for Your good. Until then, help me to use what I learned when I was there. Amen.

35

An Hour with Jesus

In the morning, O LORD, you hear my voice;
in the morning I lay my requests before you
and wait in expectation.

—Psalm 5:3

Today I am spending an hour alone with Jesus. And the sometimes elusive search for contentment of the heart comes to me as I sit in the gazebo at my alma mater. It is a gorgeous fall day, and I have come here to reminisce and reflect. I actually have an hour to sit and think and talk to God and be spoken to. I never have an hour. Or I should say, I never *take* an hour.

Jesus, I adore You. I love the way You love me right now with a cool breeze, a touch of sun, pitter-patter of water, a place to sit, and time to be blessed thoroughly. You love me sacrificially and abundantly.

Father, I adore You. You love me as a Daddy with His only daughter. You ask me to sit in Your lap. You call me by name and I run into Your arms. You love me with the sweetest and greatest love—the kind of love that never leaves or ends.

Spirit, I adore You. You love me with truth. You love me with guidance. You love me with deliberate leading (when I actually stop and listen). You love me by choosing not to leave my heart in the condition You found it. You love me boldly and purely into holiness.

I confess that my inner sanctum is a dark place worthy of investigation and in need of rearranging. I seem to think of myself first in all situations. How will I look? Come across? Be perceived? Sound? Be judged? Be criticized? Be honored? Be blessed? Be taken care of? Be fulfilled? Be significant? Be used (either good or bad)? Be changed? Be fed? Be brought down? Be encouraged? Be served? Be liked? Be loved?

- *I* want another baby.
- *I* want to live in a better neighborhood.
- *I* want my daughter to stop whining.
- *I* want my book published.
- *I* want a productive life that leaves me satisfied in my old age.
- *I* (claim to) want to be like Christ.
- *I* want . . . *I* want . . .

My, this is not a pretty picture. I am too self-motivated, self-driven, and self-absorbed. I am asking for a new perspective. I am sorry for my selfishness and for my self-pity and endless list of wants (of which only a few would likely bring You glory or thanks from me). I am sorry for the focus that rivets my gaze solely on today. I am sorry for not having more hope in my future with You. And for my faithlessness.

I thank You for loving me. I thank You for thinking of me and then creating me. I thank You for blessing me over and over and over again. I thank You, Jesus, for dying for me. What would my life look like without Your imprint, without Your blood redeeming it? I thank You for my husband—a man with a true desire for spiritual things. I thank You for Sara and Jack—my reasons for getting up each and every day. I thank You for my friends—the eyes, ears, mouths, and hands of Jesus in my life. I thank You for taking care of my every need.

And now to the part of the prayer where I give You my "wish list." You've spoken to me clearly enough just now that, fortunately, I've gained a bit of insight. This life is not about what *I* want, it's about what *You* want. And I believe this is what You want:

- to love me
- to spend time with me
- to be loved by me
- to make me holy

So that is my wish list for this moment in time. This is my prayer: Please love me; please cause me to desire and want to be with just You; please urge and enable me to love You with my heart, soul, and life; and please, please make me holy. Aren't these things what life is really all about? Amen.

Personal Touch

When was the last time you took an hour with Jesus? Put this book down, look at your calendar for this week, and write—in pen—an appointment with Jesus. And then keep it. You will not regret that use of your time.

> *But Jesus often withdrew to lonely*
> *places and prayed.*
> —Luke 5:16

Prayer

Dear Father, if You expected regular times of conversation with Your Son for His growth, then how much more do I need this time alone? It says in Your Word that You will draw near to those who draw near to You. So I ask that You honor and bless the time that I set apart. Amen.

36

Where Is Your Heart?

It should be that of your inner self,
the unfading beauty of a gentle and quiet spirit,
which is of great worth in God's sight.
—1 Peter 3:4

*I*t's not often that I, a stay-at-home wife and mom, get a
girls' day out with a thousand of my "colleagues." Last year
I attended the Hearts-at-Home conference with other women
who have been committed (sorry, Freudian slip)—who have
committed themselves to staying at home with their children during their formative years. I spent the day attending
seminars designed to professionalize our calling. I laughed;
I cried; it moved me, Bob (sorry, Veggie Tales flashback).
Seriously, though, I was touched deeply. I did laugh. I did
cry. And I was moved. In an effort to get hold of some of the
truths that sent chills through me and made me rethink my
way of being a wife and mother, I want to tell the whole
world about my struggle—or at least you, my reader. This

way, if I test myself and am found wanting, I'm now accountable to all of you for my improvement.

First my marriage skills. Here are some questions that don't easily roll off my back. These made me think and will perhaps make me act.

- At the end of _____'s (husband's name goes here) life, will his life have been better because he married me? (Whether or not our husbands have a great life depends a lot on us!)
- What has it cost (emotionally/physically/mentally/ financially) for _____ to be married to me?
- Do I live and act and speak under the truth that I am the primary "minister" to my husband?

On to my parenting. I have been challenged to think about my life. Am I restless? Is my heart surrendered to my current calling of wife and mother? Just because I am a stay-at-home mom in name does not mean that I am "there" 100 percent. Do Sara and Jack see me as torn and preoccupied, always wanting to "get just one more thing done before I ___ , honey"? (A favorite saying of my three-year-old daughter's is "Just a second, Mommy." Wonder where she picked up that little gem?) Am I wholehearted or is my heart divided? I do not know how to answer these questions, but I don't think I am always "there" with them. Have I been masking my ministry and gift development under the guise of service, of becoming all God created me to be, of keeping my sanity, or am I running away from something—from what I really need to be concentrating on right here and right now? I don't know. If that is the case, I'm still in the process of learning the logical "next step" to rectify it, if it even needs to be rectified at all.

One more juicy thought for all of you moms out there. The mother/child relationship is the strongest and longest-lasting bond in life. As I love my daughter, so she will love her children. As I love my son, so he will love his wife. My relationship with them is the prototype for all of their future love relationships. Wow . . . no pressure there. Here's the good news: It's not about where I am. It's about who God is and what He is capable of doing. I'm thankful that I have a spirit of power and love, and a sound mind—with Christ's healing and enabling—to be the healthy wife, mother, and friend that I desire and need to be.

Personal Touch

Take a moment to ask yourself the questions from above. Be prayerful, and be honest.

> *Come to me, all you who are weary and*
> *burdened, and I will give you rest.*
> —Matthew 11:28

Prayer

Father, You alone know where I place my heart each day. You alone know what treasures I am storing up in heaven and what things will pass away. Please help me see my motives and actions through Your eyes and then enable me to make any changes that You see fit. Amen.

37

The Morning from . . . Not Heaven

We will not all sleep, but we will all be changed.
—1 Corinthians 15:51

It is 9:46 A.M. on a Wednesday. Today we began potty training. Bought the seat. Bought the doll that wets itself. Bought the video. Bought the book. Bought the panties. I'm all set. Truth be told, I have no confidence whatsoever in my abilities to train my daughter in this area. And by 9:46 A.M., she has sat on the potty eight times, did not go once, but has had two accidents—one while wearing my shoes. And what a day I chose! For whatever reason, I am also attempting to make chicken pot pie for dinner for the first time. And my son has decided to dislike life very much, crawling to noncarpeted areas of the floor to lie down and clonk his head against the hardwood for dramatic effect. And, of course, my kitchen trim. Yesterday I got an urge to paint—so I did. Let me put it this way, I'll be slapping back on a coat of the old paint sometime this afternoon. My daughter just came to the top of the basement steps to implore my presence upstairs, only to tell me to "get out" as soon as she saw me. It's one of those days—and it's not even ten o'clock.

Personal Touch

Take a deep breath or two. Put yourself in the time-out chair. Make a cup of tea. Light a candle or two. Turn on an instrumental praise CD. Call a friend. Whisper to God that you need some help. Do what you need to bring some sanity to your life the next time you're having "one of those days."

> *Peace I leave with you; my peace I give you. . . .*
> *Do not let your hearts be troubled.*
> —John 14:27

Prayer

Father, get me out of here! Not really. I love my life. But I could use an "extra dose" of You and Your amazing, un-explainable peace right now. Amen.

38

True Identity

For you created my inmost being;
you knit me together in my mother's womb.
I praise You because I am fearfully and wonderfully made;
your works are wonderful,
I know that full well. . . .
All the days ordained for me
were written in your book
before one of them came to be.

—Psalm 139:13–14, 16

Scene: God knitting together human creation number 3,529,347,063 in her mother's womb.

- I will make a female.
- She will be born on September 27, 19__ (ahem).
- She will be given the name of Mary Elizabeth Klein, but will change it when she's twenty-one. It will be an independence issue.

125

- She will be born with blonde hair (and attempt to keep that color her entire life through artificial means).
- She will have her mother's green eyes and, to keep her humble, her father's nose.
- She will live through two divorces by the time she's 12. She will become stronger from the pain.
- She will be 5 feet, 3 and 3/4 inches tall, always wishing to be taller.
- She will accept the free gift of My Son and His salvation on February 4, 1986, and her name will be written in the Book of Life. She will never be the same again.
- She will hit puberty *late* (and I mean *late*). She will question My judgment at the time, but will look back and realize that she really wasn't in a hurry after all.
- She will meet the man she is to marry when she is sixteen. They will begin dating when she is eighteen, date for two years, have a broken engagement, date for another two. This, too, will only help her to depend on Me as her true companion and strength.
- She will have a slightly rebellious summer when she is twenty-one and get a rose tattoo on her ankle. I have yet to decide if I will like it or not.
- She will marry on October 15, 1993. It will be the wedding of her dreams.
- I will make her a mother on November 22, 1996, and again on June 13, 1998. I will give her the daughter she's always wanted and the son she had no idea how much she'd come to treasure. Up to this point, she's only had a glimpse of My love for her. This adds another huge piece to her puzzle.

- I will make her organized. She will thank Me on more than one occasion for the genius who invented Post-it Notes.
- I will gift her to sing and sing well. No, I change My mind. I will gift her to write, and she will thrive on that. It will go hand-in-hand with her personality.
- She will be introverted, filling up her emotional reserves with time alone and with Me.
- She will have struggles in her marriage at times. This will only cause her to be more confident in her relationship with Me as well as be more empathetic with the many different women in her life.
- I will give her a passion to minister to women. She will greatly enjoy the service opportunities I give her, wishing all Christ-followers knew what it felt like to serve within their giftedness and passions.
- Though it will take awhile, as she will have her share of scars from her earthly life, she will come to a point of accepting and even liking how I've made her. She will see her uniqueness and will want other women to see that in themselves as well.
- She is My creation.
- When she accepted Christ as her Savior, she became My daughter.
- I love her.
- She will hope all her days that her life reflects that truth.
- And when she looks back on her life, she will be able to see that it all wove together for the greater good—hers *and* Mine.

Personal Touch

Take this list and plug in your statistics and quirks and life. Let the reality of God's amazing design for your life— yes, your imperfect, struggle-filled, sometimes blah life— sink in. And look back and see His hand in as many places as you can. He has not only made you, He has created your life and has spent His time filling it with His love for you. God made you. God loves you. Yes, *you*.

> *For those God foreknew he also predestined to*
> *be conformed to the likeness of his Son.*
> —Romans 8:29

Prayer

Dear Father, You have planned my life before it even began. And You are changing me even when I don't feel it or see it. Thank You for the gift of a life that holds so many lessons and that is teaching me to be more like Your Son. Amen.

39

Dream a Little Dream for Me

For we are God's workmanship, created in Christ Jesus to do good works, which God prepared in advance for us to do.
—Ephesians 2:10

*D*reams. It's interesting that the word for the illusory, subconscious movies that we play out in our heads each night is the same word that describes the desires we want to achieve. *Dream big. Go after your dreams. She's such a dreamer.* While growing up most of us were told that we could have anything and do anything that our hearts desired, as long as we put our minds to it. Really? Can we really? What if life is not always like that? What happens when our dreams don't come true?

My mind's eye sees four kinds of people. The first are those who have no dreams—the dreamless. They are fine with just getting through life day by day—no goals, no plans, no higher aspirations. If you ask them if they are content with their lives, their eyes will glass over because they don't even understand what you're talking about.

On the other end of the spectrum are those who have spectacular, pie-in-the-sky dreams. Dreams big enough to fill two lifetimes. Dreams that keep them living in the future rather than enjoying today.

In the middle, are two others. The successful dreamers have the dreams and also have a plan of action to achieve them. They learn from the past, work in the present, and pray and strive for the future.

The last group are the part-time dreamers. They have their dreams—big dreams, even. But due to their circumstances or personality or motivation level, they cannot devote their lives to making their dreams come to pass. This is where I happen to fall right now. I have had a big dream for as long as I can remember—to write a book. However, I am a stay-at-home mom with two children under the age of two. I am a wife, a ministry leader, a friend. I have a life outside the parameters of my dream. I must make my dream happen in stages. For instance, I have written my manuscript. Stage one is complete. I now realize that was the easy part. Becoming published is the hard part, that will be a long stage. And that stage can only happen in baby steps because of my circumstances. But my dream is still there.

However, what happens when your dreams do not come true? We are told to reach for them with everything in us. We are told to pray and trust in the Lord, and He will give us the desires of our hearts (Ps. 37:4). I do not believe this means if we follow Him, He will give us anything we want. I believe the psalmist means that if we trust in Him, God will place desires into our hearts that focus us on Him. But what if we are following God and believe He has placed this desire in our hearts and, no matter how much we pray or how hard we work, our dream never comes to pass? Then what? How do we reconcile that in our minds?

I am struggling with this now as I realize my book of devotionals for young moms may sit in my hope chest and the largest audience it may reach will be my daughter when she has her first child. (Which doesn't sound so bad, actually.) But what about my dream of being published? Of publishing the book that I truly felt God cowrote with me?

I have a few thoughts on this. One, some of our dreams may not be realized this side of heaven, but may become reality when we reach the other side. (I understand that I'm taking some liberties here, but just think how many more copies I can sell there!) Two, life is not fair. I was never promised a journey where everything would go my way. Some things I want to see happen simply may not. Just because. Three, God knows my heart. He knows my prayers. He knows what I desire. But I believe He wants me to want Him more than I want my dream. Are you at that point with your particular dream? Am I?

Personal Touch

Pray for God to help you in your journey. Pray that He will speak clearly to you—through His Word, through prayer, through your circumstances, and through your church—about the dreams and plans *He* has for you. And then pray that when you do see what He wants for you, that you continue to place Him first, asking constantly for the determination and strength and dependence to make those plans come to fruition. Happy Dreaming!

Delight yourself in the Lord
and he will give you the desires of your heart.
—Psalm 37:4

Prayer

Dear Father, my dreams are beyond my life's scope. You know what they are. In fact, I believe You are the One who put them in my heart in the first place. But I have wrapped my fingers too tightly around them, so I am letting go. I am giving my dreams back to You and asking You to fulfill them only if they bring You amazing glory. Amen.

40

Woman, Be Free

A kindhearted woman gains respect.
—Proverbs 11:16

*D*o you enjoy being a woman? I mean, really enjoy it? Do you curse the day you found out where babies came from, or do you believe that childbirth is a privilege that God gave to us rather than to our male counterparts?

Women are complex, unique, deep wells that bring forth wisdom and grace. I love being a woman. I can't imagine it any other way. Women set the tone in their families, their church bodies, and their communities. Generally, we are the ones who build the deep relationships, who serve each other, who know when others need help, who see one another's struggles. We are the caretakers.

So women, just through our unique and God-given qualities, complement the vision of "seeking out the lost." Once a person comes to know Christ personally, we can take her under our wings. Once a person takes the first step toward the Cross, we can help her learn to walk with Christ. Once a person discovers her spiritual gifts, we can encourage her to serve with her giftedness.

I have many concerns for women. I want each woman to know Christ deeply and to walk with Christ consistently. I want each woman to have a strong and biblically healthy relationship with her husband. I want each woman to grow deep roots of relationships with other women, because life is hard and we need each other. I want women to serve and not grow weary, to realize that Christ's abundant life for us begins here and now. I want each woman to find contentment where she is in life—that special place she chose through God-ordained circumstances.

I want each woman to love being a woman—to see the freedom and grace and gifts that God has given each of us. I adore being a woman. I am grateful to God that I am a woman. And I wouldn't have it any other way.

Personal Touch

Do you enjoy being a woman? Sit down and list all of the pluses to our gender that you can think of, then thank God for His choice for you.

> *A woman who fears the Lord is to be praised.*
> —Proverbs 31:30

Prayer

Dear Father, being female sometimes takes its toll. So much is expected of me. I know I drop the ball a lot. Please show me why You made me a woman and how wonderfully that complements my dreams and desires. Amen.

41

Jack's Heart

Blessed are the pure in heart, for they will see God.
—Matthew 5:8

hest x-ray. EKG. Cardiologist. These words are too big for my mind's eye. They are too big for my simple life. I brought Jack in for a little cold and the doctor discovered a heart murmur. From what I understand, that in and of itself is no big deal. But combined with their perception of a low weight gain lately, tests have been ordered. There may be something wrong with my son's heart. That is beyond me. It is beyond the world that Jack and I have created—a new-found interest in Teletubbies, his obsession with Cheerios, and the way he literally bounces up and down with joy when Kevin or I walk in to get him from his crib. That is the life of my one-year-old. But it has just gotten bigger; it has just gotten scarier because there may be something wrong with his heart.

Now, of course, I am more than likely running ahead of reality by playing out the worse case scenarios in my mind.

I don't know if that's a human-thing, a woman-thing, a mom-thing, or a Beth-thing, but the worst has definitely crossed my mind. As soon as the doctor called me to tell me to set up an appointment for those big words that I mentioned a few moments ago, I instantly began to cry. Now, yes, I am emotional; yes, sometimes my emotions seem a tad out of control; and yes, I'm a mother. But this stream of tears surprised even me. After I wiped them away, I prayed, "Jesus, please give me the strength to get through this." I then changed my prayer to, "Jesus, *be* my Strength to get through this."

My life seems so simple and small and hemmed in. But I don't like the sound of those big words crashing down into my world. If it is nothing, I will thank God. But the question is, if it is *something,* will I still thank my God? I hope so, but I honestly don't know. I don't know if my faith is big enough and strong enough for something to be wrong with my precious son's heart. I hope it is. And I guess I'll find out. (Author's note: Jack is fine. It's a simple and fairly common heart murmur and nothing else.)

Personal Touch

Do you cling to your children a little more tightly than you should? I'm talking emotionally here. We need to remember something: These children that are in our care actually belong to God. We have just been given them for this season to care for and love, but we need to remind ourselves constantly to let them go and to give them to their true Parent.

*Cast all your anxiety on him because
he cares for you.*
—1 Peter 5:7

Prayer

Dear Father, it is so hard to just let go and leave my kids in Your care. It's not that I don't trust You; I don't trust this world. But I know, and I must believe, that You hold them more carefully and more closely than I ever could. Help me let them go into Your more-than-capable tending. I know You love them even more than I do, and You can parent them in holiness and perfection. Thank You for loving my children so dearly. Amen.

42

Sara Stories

Even a child is known by [her] actions,
by whether [her] conduct is pure and right.
—Proverbs 20:11

Thirty-Two Months

Dear Jesus, Sara did the sweetest thing this evening. As we sat on the stairs together, she got a dolly for herself and a bear for me. She placed the bear in my arms and said, "baby." She rocked her dolly, so I rocked the bear. She then began singing. I didn't recognize the song at first, but then I realized it was "Jesus Loves Me." I began to cry. It's been months since I rocked her and sang that to her, and I realized once again that my children are watching and listening to everything I say and do.

When Sara saw me crying, she stopped singing, put her hand on my shoulder and said, "I sorry, Mommy" (for making me cry). She is so precious and amazing, I can hardly believe I have been given this gift. Thank You for her. Amen.

Thirty-Four Months

Sara has begun thanking God for her blessings. Here is her usual order: "Thank You, Jesus, for ketchup, Kyle, rainbow, sausage, Mrs. Coakley, and Uncle John!" You've got to start somewhere.

Thirty-Five Months

New phrases:

- Umm, let me see . . . I know!
- Just a second, Mommy.
- Be nice, Jack.
- I've got a great idea!
- Thanks, *I'm* OK.
- That's not fair!

Third Birthday

The other day in a parking lot Sara would not stay close to me. After calling to her several times, and flustered with Jack dangling on my hip, I had to somewhat forcibly "drag" her to the car. A man walked past us, and Sara looked up and said to him with all the dramatic flair she could muster, "Help, mister!" I thought, "You think you need help now, kid? Just wait until we get out of view. 'Help, mister'? Who does she think she is?"

Three Plus

Kevin came home with a big empty popcorn tin and handed it to Sara to play with. She immediately set it down and banged on it like a drum. Jack tried to squeeze in for his turn and Sara pushed him away. I told Sara that she needed to share with her brother, and she said, "No, Mommy. Jack plays the guitar."

Then, a bit later, she decided the best way to elude Jack was to pick the thing up and walk away with it. She said to him as he again tried to get hold of it, "No, Jack, this is for Aunt Ruthie's birthday." (Umm, honey, Aunt Ruthie's birthday is six months from now. Nice try. Share with your brother.)

Sara has been role playing a bit lately. It's usually been that she's Mary and I'm Joseph. And when we're "in character," she will correct me if I start talking to her for real and call her Sara. The other day her baby-sitter was coming over, and we were talking about her. She left the room and came back in and said, "Hi, I'm Carrie." I said, "Hi, Carrie." She said, "Hi, Mommy." And I said, "Oh, no, if you're Carrie, then I can't be Mommy." So she said, "OK. Hi, Beth." I didn't even know she knew my name! She can be clever.

So we're driving home from church, me with the kids and Kevin on his own, and he's keeping his car next to ours to wave to the kids. We come upon a light. It turns yellow. Kevin goes through; I stop. Sara says with urgency, "We lost Daddy. He crossed a red. I can't bewieve this!"

Jack has had a great birthday, though clueless that it is indeed his birthday. However, Miss Narcissist Sara Taylor had this conversation with Kevin. Kevin said to her, "Who's birthday is it?" And she said, "Sara's birthday." And Kevin said, "No, Sara, it's Jack's birthday." And she said (in a bit of a demanding voice), "Daddy, you have to share Jack's birthday!" She even prayed tonight, "Thank You, Jesus. Thank You for giving me Jack's birthday." Amazing how the world truly does revolve around a three-year-old, huh?

Sara brings her hands together to make a shape and says, "This is a cocoon, Mommy. Cocoons are brown." And I said, "That's right, honey. Do you know who lives in a cocoon?"—knowing full well she knew the answer was "butterfly." And she says, expecting that this was the answer I must have been looking for, though I could tell she herself doubted the validity of it, "Jesus?"

So we're in the van and Kevin reaches for me as he's driving, and from the backseat Sara says, "Thank you, Daddy. Thank you for holding Mommy's hand." Wow, she's watching our every move.

Personal Touch

If you haven't already started, I urge you to keep a record of all your kids' little sayings and comings-and-goings. You'll find these happy memories will bring a smile to your face for years to come. Plus, it will be a riot to read to them when they are older!

Her children arise and call her blessed.
—Proverbs 31:28

(Blessed? We'll see about that.)

Prayer

Dear Father, write these memories on my heart. I never want to forget this time in my children's lives. Amen.

43

The End Was Inevitable

The end! The end has come.
—Ezekiel 7:2

*T*onight I am blue. After a week of fighting the end, I have been officially given the brush-off by Jack. I should clarify. I have finally allowed the little one to make his choice known. He is finished nursing, and I am sadder than I have been in quite a while. Please do not mistake my sadness for anything other than what it is. I am forever grateful that my little guy allowed me this privilege for over twenty months (much longer than I ever thought I'd even want to do it!). I am sure I am taking this so hard for two reasons: (1) This is my last child, and I haven't quite come to terms with that decision emotionally. So, unless God changes Kevin's mind and we have another baby, *or* I am appointed the wet-nurse to the child of a friend in the next week or so (I'm just kidding!), I am done nursing forever. (2) I am no longer the mother of a baby (now, technically, I could have said that probably a year ago, but there is something about nursing that allowed *me* at least to keep Jack in that "baby" stage). I am the mother of two toddlers. My babies are gone. They are a little less dependent on me each day. I don't think I was quite ready to be finished with that first stage of my mothering life. So, like I said, I am blue.

A Week Later

My, I am still quite sad. Something has occurred to me—four years ago on Leap Day, we conceived Sara. Four years and one day later, my son weaned himself. I spent four consecutive years pregnant, then nursing, then pregnant, then nursing. My heart, soul, mind, and even body spent four years straight in the baby-making, baby-carrying, baby-feeding, baby-caring years. Now they are done. I spent my entire life waiting for them to happen, and now they are all over. I must step through that next door. Yet I am resisting it so very much. My heart and soul aren't ready to leave behind that magic. My body and mind aren't ready to move ahead into aging. But something is calling me. Time is calling me. Life is calling me. And my two toddlers are calling me with hands out, waiting for me to help them learn all about God and this amazing world, and their Mommy and Daddy, and themselves. And I need to go with 100 percent of my heart and soul and body and mind, because my heavenly Father is calling me to move on. And so I must move on—fully—even if part of me is being left behind.

Personal Touch

I've heard the saying before, "The only thing that's sure in life is change." Change just keeps on coming, doesn't it?

Don't fear it. Learn to embrace it. It's usually in change that some of the best things in life come to us. And, of course, God is in ultimate control.

> *Do you know how God controls the clouds?*
> —Job 37:15

Prayer

Dear Father, You are the Planner of my life. You know when change—good and bad—is right around the corner. I ask You to please help me cultivate a heart of thankfulness and readiness for whatever You bring my way. And I pray that You assist me in holding onto precious memories, while I walk into the future with the confidence that You are in charge. Amen.

44

Build Your Life

God is the builder of everything.
—Hebrews 3:4

Dear Father,

It is time. I am tired of living in the shallow waters. My deep is calling out to Your deep. I pray to You to take me on a sacred journey—one of Christ-discovery and self-renewal. I know this is a dangerous prayer. But I am ready. I want to change and grow and stretch and learn. I want to know You better. I want to become like Christ. I want the touch of the Spirit on my life. I want to feel led in the thoughts I possess, the words I speak, the actions I take, the people I keep company with, the choices I make, the priorities I choose, the time I spend. Please live and move and have Your being in me. I am ready.

In Jesus' Name, Amen.

And so it begins. My sacred journey. I look forward to experiencing what the heavenly Father has in store for me. It is an exciting venture, this abundant life we have been so mercifully given. We are so blessed to rest in the shadow of His wings and build our lives on Him and His purposes. How exhilarating!—to know that our lives have no limits. Our Father—our actual Father—is the Creator of the universe. We have His power at our disposal. Nothing is impossible with Him. If we focus on Jesus and all that He has done for us and all that He *is* doing for us on a daily basis, everything else in our lives pales in comparison.

Personal Touch

When was the last time you felt as if you were living abundantly? Take a few moments to pray for an open heart, mind, and eyes to see what is around you. Then jot down ten things you would like to accomplish before your life here ends. Now, pray again for wisdom, discernment, and creativity. Pray that God will unleash His power in your life. You may be amazed at what He accomplishes in and through you.

Fix your thoughts on Jesus.
—Hebrews 3:1

Prayer

Dear Father, thank You for abundant life that begins now. I pray that You will help me build my life on You. I pray that You will begin a sacred journey in my heart and life today. I am ready for what You have waiting around the bend in the road. Prepare my heart by strengthening my spirit. I look forward to walking with You each day in a new and exciting way! Amen.

45

Waves of Love

Deep calls to deep
in the roar of your waterfalls;
all your waves and breakers
have swept over me.
  —Psalm 42:7

Kevin and I are on vacation. Together. Alone. I'm pretty sure that in Greek, "vacation" means "to leave the kids behind at Nana and Papa's house." We are spending five days in Michigan, and I think a part of us doesn't even know what to do with ourselves. I can't remember the last time I felt this relaxed. It's like I'm waking up after a long sleep, and I'm remembering what it's like to live as one who is unencumbered and not bound by responsibilities and time.

So, in our excursion for relaxation with no deadlines in sight, we find ourselves with a picnic dinner and a blanket trekking to a quaint beach overlooking Lake Michigan. Since you can see nothing but water touching the horizon, it might as well be an ocean. You walk up these steps and are greeted with pure beauty. It stops you dead in your tracks (especially if you're used to only the flat plains of Illinois). We just lost our breath and took it all in. Moments in time like this remind your heart how big your God really is. We showed up about seven, with the plan of dinner and sunset-watching. However, we forgot the time difference—if you can believe it, the sun doesn't go down on a summer evening in Michigan until 9:30—no kidding! So, needless to say, we had some time on our hands. But with nowhere else to go, no one to put to bed, and no baby-sitter to pay, we simply enjoyed our time. A little dinner, a walk along the beach, and a lot of just sitting and waiting for God's showing of magnificence. We sat in silence. Usually, that would have bothered me. "You mean, we've been married only seven years and have already run out of things to say?" But for some reason, I had left that way of thinking back home. And I enjoyed just being at that place, at that time, and I enjoyed the thoughts that began to wash over me.

I watched the water ebb and flow, and I heard myself saying, with each wave that reached the shore, "God loves you." Sometimes it was a larger amount of water, so I said it to myself more boldly. Sometimes it was a ripple, so it became a whisper of love. And I thought about this body of water with its ever-reaching waves as my life. Our life is nothing but a dance, a romance—God wooing us to His heart. God telling us over and over and over—never ceasing to reach out—that He loves us. The bigger waves, they may come from the wake of life's circumstances or disruptions, such as the joyful times of life or the pain-producing times of life. "It's a girl!" God *loves* you! "I don't think we should stay together." God *loves* you! Or the whispers. A song meant just for you as you turn on the radio. God *loves* you. A sunset painted as you watch. God *loves* you. A child's first soft proclamation of "I love you, Mommy." God *loves* you.

Some reaching closer to me than others, the waves kept coming and coming and coming. God never tires of the romance, never slows down His efforts to get our attention, never gives up on getting across His ultimate message—*God loves you!*

Personal Touch

When was the last time that you thought about the love of our God? I mean, really spent some time pondering the fact that He loves you completely, knowingly, attentively, quietly, compassionately, unconditionally, always? Forget your traditional quiet time activities today—put away the booklets and prayer lists—and just think about the love God has for you. Revel in it. Thank Him for it. Enjoy it today.

> *By day the* Lord *directs his love,*
> *at night his song is with me—*
> *a prayer to the God of my life.*
> —Psalm 42:8

Prayer

Dear Father, I think I forget most of the time what this life is really all about—it's simply about You loving me and me spending my entire life getting to know You better. I cannot thank You enough for pouring into me so hugely and for giving me the ultimate gift—Your absolute and unreserved love. Amen.

In Closing

*W*hen I was in high school, I began living my life with the future in mind—almost to a fault. I strove toward the next step in my goal, sometimes to the detriment of enjoying the moment. In high school, I dreamed of college and of having a boyfriend. In college, I dreamed of working full-time, living on my own, and being engaged. Once out on my own and planning a wedding, I dreamed of marriage, house, family. And here I am, in the midst of my latest dream—my own husband, my own home, my own children. And for the first time in my life, I am not wishing I were farther down the road. I'm living out my dream—as close to heaven as one can get down here. I love my life, and, with everything in me, I am doing all I can to savor each moment of this almost magical, definitely divine, existence I have been given.

I recently found an old journal that I'd kept while in college. I'd written there, "Where do I see myself in ten years? Sitting at a computer, writing a book, bouncing a baby on my lap." I laughed and I cried. How many people truly get to live out their dreams? I can hardly believe that I am.

My prayer for you, dear reader and fellow traveler, is that you embrace the chaos that is your life, and that you find your calm to get you through. He is waiting. And He will be your ever-present Help.

Enjoy the process. Enjoy the journey. Revel in your chaos and hold fast to the calm.

Resources

One of my favorite places to hang out is the World Wide Web. Here are some sites that you might enjoy, too.

Hearts-at-Home Conferences	www.hearts-at-home.org
Christian Online Mother's Group	www.justMoms.com
Marriage Partnership magazine	www.christianity.net/mp/current
Today's Christian Woman magazine	www.christianity.net/tcw/current
Christian Book Distributors	www.chrbook.com
Amazon.com—Books & Music	www.amazon.com
Women of Faith Conferences	www.women-of-faith.com
Mothers of Preschoolers	www.mops.org

I would be honored to hear from you. If you would like to contact me, you may e-mail me at:

bcorcoran@blackberrycreek.org

Thank you.

Notes

Chapter 7: Mission Incredible

1. Judith Couchman, *Designing a Woman's Life: A Bible Study and Workbook* (Sisters, Ore.: Questar Publishers, 1996), 24.

Chapter 27: Brotherly and Sisterly Love

1. Nathan Chapman, Steve Chapman, *Every Moment* (Madison, Tenn.: S&A Family, 1988).

Chapter 31: A Look Inside My Journal

1. Bill Hybels, *Too Busy Not to Pray: Slowing Down to Be with God* (Downers Grove, Ill.: InterVarsity, 1988).